Wildflowers
of
Colorado
Field Guide

by Don Mammoser
with Stan Tekiela

ADVENTURE PUBLICATIONS, INC.
CAMBRIDGE, MINNESOTA

To my wife, Shelly, who knows why - Don

To my daughter, Abigail Rose, the sweetest flower in my life - Stan

ACKNOWLEDGMENTS

Thanks to Stan Tekiela and Deborah Walsh for their help. - Don

Copy edited by Deborah Walsh

Book and icon design by Jonathan Norberg

Photo credits by photographer and page number:
Cover photo: Colorado Blue Columbine by Don Mammoser
Dudley Edmondson: 42, 54 (flower), 60, 62, 98 (flower), 230 **Mary Ellen Harte:** 138 **Richard Haug:** 222 (fruit) **Steve Olson/USDA Forest Service:** 286 (both) **Al Schneider:** 82 **Stan Tekiela:** 30, 32, 54 (fruit), 56, 98 (fruit), 118, 222 (flower), 224, 240, 274, 292, 296, 316, 332, 358, 412 **Don Mammoser:** all other photos

10 9 8 7 6 5 4 3 2
Copyright 2007 by Stan Tekiela
Published by Adventure Publications, Inc.
820 Cleveland St. S
Cambridge, MN 55008
1-800-678-7006
www.adventurepublications.net
All rights reserved
Printed in China

ISBN-13: 978-1-59193-161-4
ISBN-10: 1-59193-161-4

TABLE OF CONTENTS

COLORADO AND WILDFLOWERS

Colorado is a great place for wildflower enthusiasts! From the grassy prairies of the east to the highest mountaintops of the Rockies, Colorado is fortunate to have an extremely diverse, often unique and very healthy variety of wonderful wildflowers.

The *Wildflowers of Colorado Field Guide* is an easy-to-use field guide to help the curious nature seeker identify 200 of the most common and widespread wildflowers in Colorado. It features, with only several exceptions, the herbaceous wildflowers of Colorado. Herbaceous plants have green soft stems and die back to the ground each autumn. Only a few plants with woody stems have been included, because these particular plants are very common and have large showy flowers.

STRATEGIES FOR IDENTIFYING WILDFLOWERS

Determining the color of the flower is the first step in a simple five-step process to identify a wildflower.

Because this field guide is organized by color, identifying an unknown wildflower is as simple as matching the color of the flower to the color section of the book. The color tabs on each page identify the color section.

The second step in determining the identity of a wildflower is the size. Within each color section the flowers are arranged by the size of the flower, or flower cluster, from small to large. A plant with a single small yellow flower will be in the beginning of the yellow section, while a large white flower will be toward the end of the white section. Sometimes flowers are made up of many individual flowers in clusters that are perceived to be one larger flower. Therefore, these will be ordered by the size of the cluster, not the individual flower. Sections may also incorporate the average size in a range. See page 428 for rulers to help estimate flower and leaf sizes.

Once you have determined the color and approximate size, observe the appearance of the flower. Is it a single flower or cluster of flowers? If it is a cluster, is the general shape of the cluster flat, round or spike? For the single flowers, note if the flower has a regular, irregular, bell or tube shape. Also, counting the number of petals might help to identify these individual flowers. Compare your findings with the descriptions on each page. Examining the flower as described above should reduce identification possibilities of the wildflower to a few candidates.

The fourth step is to look at the leaves. There are several possible shapes or types of leaves. Simple leaves have only one leaf blade, but can be lobed. Compound leaves have a long central leafstalk with many smaller leaflets attached. Twice compound leaves have at least two leafstalks and many leaflets. Sometimes it is helpful to note if the leaves have an edge (margin) that is toothed or smooth, so look for this also.

For the fifth step, check to see how the leaf is attached to the stem. Some plants may look similar, but have different leaf attachments, so this can be very helpful. Look to see if the leaves are attached opposite of each other along the stem, alternately, or whorled around a point on the stem. Sometimes the leaves occur at the base of the plant (basal). Some leaves do not have a leafstalk and clasp the stem at their base (clasping). In other cases, the stem appears to pass through the base of the leaf (perfoliate).

Using these five steps (color, size, shape, leaves and leaf attachment) will help you gather the clues needed to quickly and easily identify the common wildflowers of Colorado.

USING THE ICONS

Sometimes the botanical terms for leaf type, attachment and type of flower can be confusing and difficult to remember. Because of this, we have included icons at the bottom of each page. They can be used to quickly and visually match the main features of the plant to the specimen you are viewing without needing to completely understand the botanical terms. By using the photos, text descriptions and icons in this field guide, you should be able to quickly and easily identify most of the common wildflowers of Colorado.

The icons are arranged from left to right in the following order: flower cluster type, flower type, leaf type, leaf attachment and fruit. The first two flower icons refer to cluster type and flower type. While these are not botanically separate categories, we have made separate icons for them to simplify identification.

FLOWER CLUSTER ICONS

    (icon color is dependent on flower color)

Flat   **Round**   **Spike**

Clusters (collections) of flowers can be categorized into one of three cluster types based on its overall shape. The flat, round and spike types refer to the cluster shape, which is easy to observe. Technically, there is another cluster type, composite, which appears as a single daisy-like flower, but is actually a cluster of many tiny flowers. Because this is often perceived as a flower type, we have included the icon in the flower type section. See page 9 for its description.

See page 9 for its description.

Some examples of cluster types

Flat   Round   Spike

FLOWER TYPE ICONS

       (icon color is dependent on flower color)

Regular   **Irregular**   **Composite**   **Bell**   **Tube**

Botanically speaking, there are many types of flowers, but in this guide, we are simplifying them to five basic types. Regular flowers are defined as having a round shape with three or more petals, lacking a disk-like center. Irregular flowers are not round, but uniquely shaped with fused petals. Bell flowers are hanging with fused petals. Tube flowers are longer and narrower than bell flowers and point up. Composite flowers (technically a flower cluster) are usually compact round clusters of tiny flowers appearing as one larger flower.

Some examples of flower types

Regular   Irregular   Bell

Tube   Composite

disk flowers
ray flowers

Composite cluster: Although a composite flower is technically a type of flower cluster, we are including the icon in the flower type category, since most people unfamiliar with botany would see it as a separate flower type. A composite flower consists of petals (ray flowers) and/or a round disk-like center (disk flowers). Sometimes a flower has only ray flowers, sometimes only disk flowers, or both.

LEAF TYPE ICONS

Simple

Simple Lobed

Compound

Twice Compound

Palmate

Leaf type can be broken down into two main types: simple and compound. Simple leaves are leaves that are in one piece; the leaf is not divided into smaller leaflets. It can have teeth or be smooth along the edges. The simple leaf is depicted by the simple icon. Simple leaves may have lobes and sinuses that give the leaf a unique shape. These simple leaves with lobes are depicted by the simple lobed icon.

Some examples of leaf types

Simple   Simple Lobed

Compound   Twice Compound   Palmate

Compound leaves have two or more distinct small leaves, called leaflets, arising from a single stalk. In this book we are dividing compound leaves into regular compound, twice compound or palmate compound leaves. Twice compound leaves are those with many distinct leaflets that arise from a secondary leafstalk. Palmate compound leaves are those with three or more leaflets arising from a common central point.

LEAF ATTACHMENT ICONS

Alternate   **Opposite**   **Whorl**   **Perfoliate**   **Clasping**   **Basal**

Leaves attach to the stems in different ways for different plants. Check to see where and how each leaf is attached to the main stem. There are six main types of attachment, as indicated, but sometimes a plant can have two different types of attachments. This is most often seen in the combination of basal leaves and leaves that attach along the main stem, either alternate or opposite (cauline leaves). These wildflowers have some leaves at the base of the plant, usually in a rosette pattern, and some leaves along the stem. In these cases, both icons are presented. For most plants there will only be one leaf attachment icon.

Some examples of leaf attachment

Alternate   Opposite   Whorl

Perfoliate   Clasping   Basal

Alternate leaves attach to the stem in an alternating pattern, while opposite leaves attach to the stem directly opposite from each other. Whorled leaves have three or more leaves that attach around the stem at the same point. Perfoliate leaves are also stalkless and have a leaf base that completely surrounds the main stem. Clasping leaves have no stalk and the base of the leaf partly surrounds the main stem. Basal leaves are those that originate at the base of a plant, near the ground, usually grouped in a round rosette.

FRUIT ICONS

Berry

Pod

(icon color is dependent on fruit color at maturity)

In some flower descriptions a fruit category has been included. This may be especially useful when a plant is not in bloom or when the fruit is particularly large or otherwise noteworthy. Botanically speaking, there are many types of fruit. We have simplified these often confusing fruit categories into two general groups, berry and pod.

Some examples of fruit types

Berry   Pod

The berry icon is used to depict a soft, fleshy, often round structure containing seeds. The pod icon is used to represent a dry structure that, when mature, splits open to release seeds.

SEASON OF BLOOM

Most wildflowers have a specific season of blooming. You probably won't see, for example, the common spring-blooming Sand Lily blooming in summer or fall. Knowing the season of bloom can help you narrow your selection as you try to identify an unknown flower. In this field guide, spring usually means April, May and the first half of June. Summer refers to the last half of June, July and August. Fall usually means September and October.

LIFE CYCLE/ORIGIN

The life cycle of a wildflower describes how long a wildflower lives. Annual wildflowers are short-lived. They sprout, grow and bloom in only one season, never to return except from seed. Most wildflowers have perennial life cycles that last many years. Perennial wildflowers are usually deeply rooted plants that grow from the roots each year. They return each year from their roots, but they also produce seeds to start other perennial plants. Similar to the annual life cycle is the biennial life cycle. This group of plants takes two seasons of growth to bloom. In the first year, the plant produces a low growth of basal leaves. During the second year, the plant sends up a flower stalk from which it produces seeds for starting new plants. However, the original plant will not return for a third year of growth.

Origin indicates whether the plants are native or non-native. Most of the wildflowers in this book originate in Colorado and are considered native plants. Non-native plants were frequently introduced unintentionally when they escaped from gardens or farms. Most non-native plants are now naturalized in Colorado.

LIFE ZONES/HABITATS

Sometimes noting the habitat surrounding a flower in question can be a clue to its identity. In Colorado, there are five distinct life zones, namely plains, foothills, montane, subalpine and alpine. These life zones are based upon ranges of elevation and changes in plant and animal life. Some plants are only found in certain life zones; others are generalists and can be found in more than one zone or even in all five.

Elevations of 3,500-6,000 feet (1,065-1,830 m) are considered plains. The trees in this life zone grow primarily on the banks of rivers and streams. Shrubs, yucca and cacti can be seen in open grasslands, which are rich with wildflowers.

Dry shrubs and woodlands with trees such as Gambel Oaks, Pinyon Pines and junipers characterize the foothills, which range from 6,000-8,000 feet (1,830-2,440 m). Ponderosa Pines, Colorado Spruces and aspen groves are also found here. Wildflowers in the foothills are common and diverse.

The montane zone ranges from 8,000-10,000 feet (2,440-3,050 m) and is the one of two forested zones in Colorado. Huge conifer forests, which include Douglas Firs, Lodgepole Pines and Ponderosa Pines, dominate the hills and valleys. Aspen groves can be enormous, adding character to the montane environment. Open areas and the shady habitats beneath forest canopies (understories) provide a lush environment for many wildflowers.

Like the montane, the subalpine zone is also densely forested, but at higher elevations of 10,000-12,000 feet (3,050-3,660 m). Some aspens and even Bristlecone Pines are mixed in with the dominant spruce and fir trees. Water (snow and summer runoff) is abundant here, giving rise to lush meadows and carpets of wildflowers.

The timberline, the upper limit of elevation above which trees do not grow, divides the subalpine and alpine zones. It varies geographically–in northern Colorado it can be as low as 11,000 feet (3,350 m), while it may be as high as 12,000 feet (3,660 m) in the southern part of the state. The alpine zone (commonly called tundra) is above the timberline and ranges up to 14,000 feet (4,270 m). Characterized by harsh, freezing winters with hurricane force winds and short summer growing seasons, it is a tough environment in which to survive. Plants here must germinate, grow, flower and reproduce–all in a few weeks. Visitors to the tundra, whose timing is right, will view an unbelievably beautiful display of wildflowers.

RANGE

The wide variety of life zones in Colorado naturally restricts the range of certain wildflowers that have specific requirements. Sometimes this section can help you eliminate a wildflower from consideration based solely on its range. However, please keep in mind that the ranges indicate where the flower is most commonly found. They are general guidelines only and there will certainly be exceptions to these ranges.

NOTES

The Notes are fun and fact-filled with many gee-whiz tidbits of interesting information such as historical uses, other common names, insect relationship, color variations and much more. Much of the information in this section cannot be found in other wildflower field guides.

CAUTION

In the Notes, it is mentioned that in some cultures, some of the wildflowers were used for medicine or food. While some find this interesting, DO NOT use this guide to identify edible or medicinal plants. Some of the wildflowers in Colorado are toxic or have toxic look-alikes that can cause severe problems. Do not take the chance of making a mistake. Please enjoy the wildflowers with your eyes, nose or with your camera. In addition, please don't pick, trample or transplant any wildflowers you see. The flower of a plant is its reproductive structure, and if you pick a flower you have eliminated its ability to reproduce. Transplanting wildflowers is another destructive occurrence. Most wildflowers need specific soil types, pH levels or special bacteria or fungi in the soil to grow properly. If you attempt to transplant a wildflower to a habitat that is not suitable for its particular needs, the wildflower most likely will die. Also, some wildflowers, due to their dwindling populations, are protected by laws that forbid you to harm the plants in any way. The good news is many of our Colorado wildflowers are now available at local garden centers. These wildflowers have been cultivated and have not been dug from the wild.

Enjoy the Wild Wildflowers!

Don and Stan

COMMON NAME
Scientific name

Family: common family name (scientific family name)

Height: average range of mature plant **Color indicator** ↗

Flower: general information such as color, size of flower or flower cluster, may include flower type, number of petals or description of flower stem

Leaf: general information such as shape and size, may include color, lobes, leaflets, teeth, veins, attachment or leafstalk

Fruit: berry or pod, including shape, color and size

Bloom: season(s) when flower blooms

Cycle/Origin: annual, perennial, biennial, native or non-native

Zone/Habitat: plains, foothills, montane, subalpine, alpine; places where found, may include soil types or sun/shade preferences

Range: throughout or part of Colorado where found

Notes: Helpful identification information, history, origin and other interesting gee-whiz nature facts.

Not all icons are found on every page.
See preceding pages for icon descriptions.

CLUSTER TYPE	FLOWER TYPE	LEAF TYPE	LEAF ATTACHMENT	FRUIT
Spike	Regular	Simple	Alternate	Berry

ALPINE FORGET-ME-NOT
Eritrichium nanum

Family: Borage (Boraginaceae)

Height: 1-2" (2.5-5 cm)

Flower: bright blue (rarely white), ¼" (.6 cm) wide, made up of 5 petals surrounding a white center and yellow throat

Leaf: tiny, less than ¼" (.6 cm) long, silvery white; leaves densely clustered beneath the flowers

Fruit: smooth hairless green nutlet, turning brown

Bloom: summer

Cycle/Origin: perennial, native

Zone/Habitat: alpine; open slopes, rocky ridges

Range: western half of Colorado

Notes: Found growing on many Colorado mountain peaks, seeing a blooming Alpine Forget-me-not upon reaching a summit is truly a reward. Like most successful tundra plants, it grows low to avoid the harsh winds, and one must get down on hands and knees to detect its delicate fragrance. This plant rarely has white flowers with yellow throats. Genus name *Eritrichium* is derived from the Greek *erion* for "wool" and *trichos* for "hair," and refers to the hairy leaves. The latter part of the common name comes from the story of a suitor who reached too far over a cliff to obtain a flower for his love, fell and cried out, "Forget me not!"

FLOWER TYPE	LEAF TYPE	LEAF ATTACHMENT	LEAF ATTACHMENT	FRUIT
Regular	Simple	Alternate	Basal	Pod

PARRY BELLFLOWER
Campanula parryi

Family: Bellflower (Campanulaceae)

Height: 4-8" (10-20 cm)

Flower: blue to light purple, ½-¾" (1-2 cm) long, 5 petals are fused together at the base to form a tube; looks funnel-shaped, sitting erect (sometimes tilted) atop a flower stem

Leaf: thin and stalked lower, 2-3" (5-7.5 cm) long; stalk-less upper (cauline); both types alternately attached

Fruit: green capsule, turning brown, ⅙-½" (.4-1 cm) long

Bloom: summer

Cycle/Origin: perennial, native

Zone/Habitat: montane, subalpine; moist sites, meadows, slopes

Range: western half of Colorado

Notes: At first glance, this plant can be confused with Harebell (pg. 115), but a second look at the single upright, funnel-shaped flower atop the stalk is a good indication you have found a Parry Bellflower. Some flowers look like an upside-down bell, as the latter part of the common name suggests. Named after Charles Parry, a nineteenth century explorer of the West. Also known as Purple Bellflower or Parry Harebell. The Navajo Indians used dried crushed leaves and stems to help heal wounds.

FLOWER TYPE	LEAF TYPE	LEAF ATTACHMENT	FRUIT
Tube	Simple	Alternate	Pod

TALL FRINGED BLUEBELLS
Mertensia ciliata

Family: Borage (Boraginaceae)

Height: 2-5' (60-150 cm)

Flower: blue, ½-¾" (1-2 cm) long, with 5 petals fused together to form a narrow bell; in nodding groups

Leaf: lance-shaped, up to 6" (15 cm) long, smooth, alternately attached; stalked lower leaves, stalkless upper leaves (cauline)

Fruit: wrinkled green nutlet, turning brown with age, ¼" (.6 cm) long

Bloom: spring, summer

Cycle/Origin: perennial, native

Zone/Habitat: montane; moist meadows, along streams and ponds

Range: western half of Colorado

Notes: Also known as Mountain Bluebells or Tall Chiming Bells, this wildflower grows abundantly in wet or moist mountainous areas and forms dense pockets of lush vegetation. Often attains a height of over 4 feet (120 cm). Its unopened flowers are nearly red, turning blue as they bloom. The genus *Mertensia* is named after the German botanist Franz Mertens. Deer, elk and bear eat the large soft leaves. Some American Indian tribes cooked and ate the young leaves or used them as a seasoning.

FLOWER TYPE	LEAF TYPE	LEAF ATTACHMENT	FRUIT
Bell	Simple	Alternate	Pod

PRAIRIE BLUEBELLS
Mertensia lanceolata

Family: Borage (Boraginaceae)

Height: 8-12" (20-30 cm)

Flower: blue, ¾" (2 cm) long, made up of 5 petals fused together to form a narrow bell; flowers arranged in nodding groups

Leaf: lance-shaped, 2-4" (5-10 cm) long, usually erect, light green, soft, toothless, alternately attached

Bloom: spring

Cycle/Origin: perennial, native

Zone/Habitat: plains, foothills, montane; dry slopes, openings in forests

Range: throughout

Notes: One of the first wildflowers to bloom each spring, Prairie Bluebells sprout when the winter snow has mostly melted and the days become warm. Prefers somewhat dry habitats and prairie slopes. Will grow singly or in small bunches, but never attains the height, mass or abundance of its close relative, Tall Fringed Bluebells (pg. 23). Its tall leaning stems have alternately attached leaves that usually point upward. The species name *lanceolata* refers to the lance-shaped leaves. Flowers attract pollinators such as bees, moths and butterflies.

FLOWER TYPE	LEAF TYPE	LEAF ATTACHMENT
Bell	Simple	Alternate

WESTERN BLUE FLAX
Linum lewisii

Family: Flax (Linaceae)

Height: 1-3' (30-90 cm)

Flower: light blue (shade varies), ¾-1" (2-2.5 cm) wide, saucer-shaped, composed of 5 delicate petals that surround a group of yellowish flower parts

Leaf: narrow, 1" (2.5 cm) long, thin, alternately attached

Fruit: round green capsule, turning brown

Bloom: spring, summer

Cycle/Origin: perennial, native

Zone/Habitat: all life zones except alpine; open sites, dry hills and fields

Range: throughout

Notes: The casual observer may be confused by the blooming habit of Western Blue Flax. In the morning, the plant may be full of blooms, but the same plant will appear to have no flowers in the afternoon since they fade or fall off the plant as the day progresses. Grows in large groups of wiry-stemmed plants that shake with the slightest wind. American Indians used the long, tough stem fibers for ropes, cords, fishing lines and nets. Also called Wild Flax or Prairie Flax. This plant makes a great addition to flower gardens because its blooming cycle persists for many weeks.

FLOWER TYPE	LEAF TYPE	LEAF ATTACHMENT	FRUIT
Regular	**Simple**	**Alternate**	**Pod**

27

CHICORY
Cichorium intybus

Family: Aster (Asteraceae)

Height: 1-4' (30-120 cm)

Flower: sky blue, 1¼" (3 cm) wide, composed of up to 20 square-tipped, fringed petals (ray flowers); stalkless flowers sparsely populate a tall stem; sometimes color ranges from white to pink, depending upon age and location

Leaf: dandelion-like, 3-6" (7.5-15 cm) long, toothed and basally attached; oblong stem leaf (cauline) is much smaller, ½-1" (1-2.5 cm) long, lacks teeth and clasps the stem

Bloom: summer, fall

Cycle/Origin: perennial, non-native

Zone/Habitat: plains; dry soils, along roads, open fields, sun

Range: throughout

Notes: Also known as Blue Sailor or Ragged Sailor. Its few flowers open one at a time, close by early afternoon and last only one day. This European import (believed to come from Eurasia) was brought to the U.S. to be cultivated for its long taproot, which can be dug up, roasted and ground to be used as a coffee substitute or additive. Like dandelion leaves, its edible leaves are high in vitamins and minerals, but taste quite bitter.

FLOWER TYPE	LEAF TYPE	LEAF ATTACHMENT	LEAF ATTACHMENT	LEAF ATTACHMENT
Composite	**Simple**	**Alternate**	**Clasping**	**Basal**

PRAIRIE SPIDERWORT
Tradescantia occidentalis

Family: Spiderwort (Commelinaceae)

Height: 10-24" (25-60 cm)

Flower: blue to rose (sometimes pink to white), 1-2" (2.5-5 cm) wide, 3 petals surrounding a golden yellow center; in a cluster of up to 10 flowers, opening only a few at a time

Leaf: grass-like, 15" (38 cm) long, folded lengthwise to form a V groove, clasps the stem

Bloom: spring, summer

Cycle/Origin: perennial, native

Zone/Habitat: plains, foothills; dry soils, sandy ridges, meadows, fields, along roads

Range: eastern half of Colorado

Notes: Unusual-looking plant with exotic-looking flowers. Flowers open in the morning and often wilt by noon on hot days. "Spider" in the common name comes from several characteristics unique to the plant. One is the angular leaf attachment, suggestive of the legs of a sitting spider; another is the stringy, mucilaginous sap that strings out like a spider's web when the leaf is torn apart. "Wort" is derived from *wyrt*, an Old English word for "plant." The genus name *Tradescantia* is in honor of J. Tradescant, an English gardener.

FLOWER TYPE	LEAF TYPE	LEAF ATTACHMENT	LEAF ATTACHMENT
Regular	Simple	Alternate	Clasping

PASQUEFLOWER
Anemone patens

Family: Buttercup (Ranunculaceae)

Height: 4-10" (10-25 cm)

Flower: pale blue to white (rarely purple), 1-2" (2.5-5 cm) wide, 5-7 petal-like sepals surround a yellow center; grows on a single, densely haired stem

Leaf: deeply divided with very narrow lobes, ⅛" (.3 cm) wide, on long stalks, basally attached; stalkless whorled leaves present just beneath the flower; both types covered with long silky hairs that makes them look gray

Bloom: early spring

Cycle/Origin: perennial, native

Zone/Habitat: all life zones; dry soils, prairies, sun

Range: throughout

Notes: All parts of Pasqueflower contain poisonous compounds; contact with this plant can cause blisters on the sensitive mucus membranes in the nose and mouth. Also called Prairie Crocus, the Pasqueflower is one of the earliest plants to bloom in Colorado. The entire plant (including flowers) is covered with soft silvery hairs that may trap warm air next to the plant in the cool spring air. Common name is derived from its blooming time, often during the Easter (Paschal) season. The seed-like fruit has feathery, plume-like hairs, 1-2 inches (2.5-5 cm) long, that carry seeds away on the wind.

FLOWER TYPE	LEAF TYPE	LEAF ATTACHMENT	LEAF ATTACHMENT

Regular	Simple Lobed	Whorl	Basal

COLORADO BLUE COLUMBINE
Aquilegia coerulea

Family: Buttercup (Ranunculaceae)

Height: 8-36" (20-90 cm)

Flower: pale blue to white, 3" (7.5 cm) long, bell-shaped, composed of 5 petals with long blue spurs and 5 petal-like sepals that are pale to sky blue

Leaf: twice compound, divided into 3 leaflets on slender stalks; each leaflet, 2-4" (5-10 cm) wide, 3-lobed, basally attached; upper leaves are much smaller and stalkless

Fruit: hairy light brown pod, 1¼" (3 cm) long

Bloom: summer

Cycle/Origin: perennial, native

Zone/Habitat: all life zones except plains; rocky slopes, clearings in forests, damp ravines, aspen groves

Range: western half of Colorado

Notes: This spectacular wildflower is quite deserving of the honor of being Colorado's state flower. "Columbine" comes from the Latin word *colum*, for "dove," referring to the flower petals resembling a group of birds in flight. The species name *coerulea* means "blue." An important nectar source for several hummingbird species in the state. Often cultivated successfully in flower gardens from seed. Do not pick the flowers or transplant it from its wild habitat, as this plant is a protected species.

FLOWER TYPE	LEAF TYPE	LEAF ATTACHMENT	FRUIT
Bell	Twice Compound	Basal	Pod

TEASEL
Dipsacus fullonum

Family: Teasel (Dipsacaceae)

Height: 2-6' (60-180 cm)

Flower: ovate-to-round cluster, 1-3" (2.5-7.5 cm) long, of many small blue-lavender flowers; each flower, ½" (1 cm) long, tightly arranged on flower head; long pointed bracts at base of flower head

Leaf: lance-shaped, 4-16" (10-40 cm) long, toothed, clasping the stem; upper leaves fused together at the stem (perfoliate)

Bloom: summer, fall

Cycle/Origin: biennial, non-native

Zone/Habitat: plains, foothills, montane; roadsides, old fields, disturbed soils

Range: throughout

Notes: A tall plant with thistle-like spines on the stem. The flower heads dry nicely, lasting well into winter, and are sometimes used in dried flower arrangements. A non-native plant that was brought from Europe. The dried heads were cultivated by wool companies, fixed as spindles and used to raise the nap (tease) of wool cloth, hence the common name. There are over 250 species of teasel, and all are native to the Old World.

CLUSTER TYPE	FLOWER TYPE	LEAF TYPE	LEAF ATTACHMENT	LEAF ATTACHMENT	LEAF ATTACHMENT
Round	Tube	Simple	Opposite	Perfoliate	Clasping

BLUE VERVAIN
Verbena hastata

Family: Vervain (Verbenaceae)

Height: 2-6' (60-180 cm)

Flower: tall thin spike cluster, 2-4" (5-10 cm) long, of deep blue flowers; each tiny flower, ⅛" (.3 cm) long, made of 5 petals that fuse at the base to form a short tube

Leaf: narrowly lance-shaped, 4-6" (10-15 cm) long, toothed, oppositely attached; lower leaves are sometimes 3-lobed

Bloom: summer

Cycle/Origin: perennial, native

Zone/Habitat: plains, foothills; wet soils, along ditches, shores, wet fields, roadsides

Range: eastern half of Colorado

Notes: Blue Vervain is a tall slender plant with multiple, pencil-thin flower spikes that bloom from the bottom up. Its stems are square with opposite leaves, which is why it is often confused with a member of the Mint family. In ancient times it was thought the plant had medicinal properties, giving rise to the genus name *Verbena,* Latin for "sacred plant." This plant rarely produces a pink flower. Its flowers are visited by many butterflies and bees for their high nectar content.

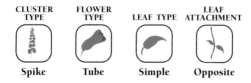

CLUSTER TYPE	FLOWER TYPE	LEAF TYPE	LEAF ATTACHMENT
Spike	Tube	Simple	Opposite

SILVERY LUPINE
Lupinus argenteus

Family: Pea or Bean (Fabaceae)

Height: 12-30" (30-76 cm)

Flower: dense spike cluster, 2-8" (5-20 cm) long, of deep blue-to-purple (rarely white) flowers; each flower, ½" (1 cm) long, pea-like, 2 petals (lips)

Leaf: divided into 5-9 leaflets, 1-2½" (2.5-6 cm) long, covered with dense silvery hairs; leaves are alternately attached

Fruit: elongated green seedpod, turning brown with age, 1½" (4 cm) long; pod is bean-like and hairy

Bloom: summer

Cycle/Origin: perennial, native

Zone/Habitat: foothills, montane, subalpine; in forest openings, along roads, hillsides

Range: western half of Colorado

Notes: Named Silver Lupine for the fine hairs that cover the leaves, stems and seedpods, giving the plant a silvery appearance. Also known as the Common Lupine. There are about 600 species of lupines in North America and many do hybridize, making positive identification difficult. The flowers and seeds of some lupines are poisonous, thus no part of any lupine should ever be eaten. A host plant for many butterflies including sulphurs, hairstreaks and blues.

CLUSTER TYPE

Spike

FLOWER TYPE

Irregular

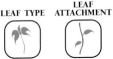

LEAF TYPE

Palmate

LEAF ATTACHMENT

Alternate

FRUIT

Pod

CREEPING BELLFLOWER
Campanula rapunculoides

Family: Bellflower (Campanulaceae)

Height: 1-3' (30-90 cm)

Flower: spike cluster, 4-8" (10-20 cm) long, of soft blue, bell-shaped flowers; each flower, 1-2" (2.5-5 cm) long, composed of 5 sharply pointed petals fused together to form a bell; flowers are on only one side of tall stem and almost always point downward

Leaf: heart-shaped, 2" (5 cm) wide, on lower part of stem; lance-shaped, ½-1" (1-2.5 cm) long, finely toothed, on upper part of stem

Fruit: downward-drooping, pod-like green container, turning light brown; holds many tiny seeds

Bloom: summer, fall

Cycle/Origin: perennial, non-native

Zone/Habitat: plains, foothills, montane; dry soils, fields, old homesteads, sun

Range: throughout

Notes: Although native to Eurasia, Creeping Bellflower is also called European Bellflower and was undoubtedly introduced to the U.S. through Europe. A common garden plant 30-50 years ago, it escaped cultivation and can now be found growing in the wild near old homesteads and abandoned gardens. Spreads by underground stems and, once established, is often difficult to eliminate.

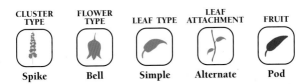

CLUSTER TYPE	FLOWER TYPE	LEAF TYPE	LEAF ATTACHMENT	FRUIT
Spike	Bell	Simple	Alternate	Pod

PINEAPPLEWEED
Matricaria discoidea

Family: Aster (Asteraceae)

Height: 3-8" (7.5-20 cm)

Flower: green to yellow, ¼" (.6 cm) long, dome-shaped; several (often many) tiny flowers near top of plant

Leaf: parsley-like, ½-1" (1-2.5 cm) long; leaf is highly divided into thin leaflets

Bloom: summer, fall

Cycle/Origin: annual, native

Zone/Habitat: foothills, montane; dry soils, along roads, disturbed soils, farmyards, sun

Range: western half of Colorado

Notes: A small inconspicuous plant that grows in disturbed soils along sidewalks, roads and gardens. Pineappleweed is so named because its flowers and leaves smell strongly of pineapple when crushed. The flower heads also makes a delicious yellow tea. A type of aster, it has a composite flower of disk flowers only, lacking petals (ray flowers). Pineappleweed is a close relative of Scentless Chamomile (pg. 233), which has white, daisy-like ray flowers that surround yellow disk flowers.

FLOWER TYPE	LEAF TYPE	LEAF ATTACHMENT
Composite	Simple Lobed	Alternate

BIG SAGEBRUSH
Artemisia tridentata

Family: Aster (Asteraceae)

Height: 2-10' (60-300 cm); shrub

Flower: spike cluster, 1-4" (2.5-10 cm) long, of tiny pale green-to-pale yellow flowers; flowers appear darker yellow in late fall when they are laden with pollen

Leaf: wedge-shaped, 1-1½" (2.5-4 cm) long, grayish green, 3-lobed tip, alternately attached

Bloom: summer, fall

Cycle/Origin: perennial, native

Zone/Habitat: all life zones except alpine; dry hillsides, deserts, open slopes

Range: throughout

Notes: Big Sagebrush has a wonderful scent that some call "the smell of the West." It is the most common grayish green shrub in Colorado. Found throughout the state, it sometimes ranges over hundreds of square miles of open areas. Look for the wedge-shaped leaves with 3-lobed tips of this evergreen plant to help identify. The branches and stems often peel and shred, adding important organic matter to the soil. American Indians ate the dried seeds either ground up into a meal or cooked.

CLUSTER TYPE	FLOWER TYPE	LEAF TYPE	LEAF ATTACHMENT
Spike	**Composite**	**Simple**	**Alternate**

FOXTAIL BARLEY
Hordeum jubatum

Family: Grass (Poaceae)

Height: 1-2' (30-60 cm)

Flower: nodding spike cluster, 2-4" (5-10 cm) long, made up of tiny green flowers; each flower, ⅛" (.3 cm) long; flowers lacks petals, but project many slender bristles; green bristles turn purplish, then tan

Leaf: slender, up to 6" (15 cm) long, parallel veins, clasps the stem

Bloom: summer

Cycle/Origin: perennial, native

Zone/Habitat: plains, foothills, montane; open areas, disturbed sites, along roads, moist meadows

Range: throughout

Notes: Clumps of Foxtail Barley shimmering in the sun and swaying in the breezes can be seen in abundance along Colorado roadsides. Flower cluster resembles the bushy tail of a fox, hence the first part of its common name. Dried seed heads are prickly and can cause injuries to the mouths, noses and eyes of grazing animals, and Navajo Indians believed they could kill a human if they got into the mouth.

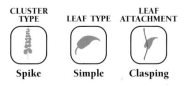

CLUSTER TYPE — **Spike**   LEAF TYPE — **Simple**   LEAF ATTACHMENT — **Clasping**

ORANGE AGOSERIS
Agoseris aurantiaca

Family: Aster (Asteraceae)

Height: 4-24" (10-60 cm)

Flower: orange (sometimes yellow), 1" (2.5 cm) wide, made up of many overlapping petals (ray flowers), lacking center disk flowers; sits atop a leafless stalk

Leaf: narrow and grass-like, up to 12" (30 cm) long, basally attached, sometimes with a few large teeth

Bloom: summer

Cycle/Origin: perennial, native

Zone/Habitat: all life zones except plains; dry soils, open areas in forests, along roads, hillsides

Range: western half of Colorado

Notes: Also known as Burnt Orange Dandelion, since it looks very similar to and sometimes shares the yellow color of the Common Dandelion (pg. 317). Insects pollinate the flowers, which have both male and female flower parts (monoecious). An infusion made from the plant parts was once used to treat wounds. The flower stalks and leaves contain a milky sap called latex. American Indians chewed the leaves like gum because of the rubbery compounds in the sap.

FLOWER TYPE	LEAF TYPE	LEAF ATTACHMENT
Composite	Simple Lobed	Basal

ORANGE PAINTBRUSH
Castilleja integra

Family: Snapdragon (Scrophulariaceae)

Height: 8-14" (20-36 cm)

Flower: spike cluster, 1-3" (2.5-7.5 cm) long, composed of inconspicuous green flowers interspersed among bright reddish orange bracts; bracts often mistaken for the flower petals

Leaf: long and narrow, 1-3" (2.5-7.5 cm) long, edges usually curl upward along entire length of the leaf, alternately attached

Fruit: elongated pod-like green container, turning brown, ¾" (2 cm) long; contains seeds

Bloom: spring, summer

Cycle/Origin: perennial, native

Zone/Habitat: plains, foothills; open hillsides, rocky slopes

Range: eastern half of Colorado

Notes: A very common and beautiful plant in the foothills and plains of Colorado. Sometimes grows in large, extremely showy clumps. "Paintbrush" refers to the flowers, which look like the used brushes of a painter. Most paintbrushes are semiparasitic–their roots cling to those of nearby plants to absorb nutrients. Attracts hummingbirds, which use their long tongues to reach the nectar deep inside the green flowers. In turn, hummingbirds help pollinate the flowers. Also called Wholeleaf Indian Paintbrush.

CLUSTER TYPE	FLOWER TYPE	LEAF TYPE	LEAF ATTACHMENT	FRUIT
Spike	Tube	Simple	Alternate	Pod

fruit

BUTTERFLYWEED
Asclepias tuberosa

Family: Milkweed (Asclepiadaceae)

Height: 1-2' (30-60 cm)

Flower: large flat cluster, 2-3" (5-7.5 cm) wide, of small orange flowers; each flower, ⅜" (.9 cm) wide, has downward-curved petals; color can vary from all yellow to red

Leaf: lance-shaped, 2-6" (5-15 cm) long, toothless, hairy, widens near tip

Fruit: erect narrow green pod, turning brown with age, 6" (15 cm) long, covered with fine hairs; pods in small clusters and have large brown seeds with silken "parachutes" to carry away each seed

Bloom: spring, summer

Cycle/Origin: perennial, native

Zone/Habitat: plains, foothills; dry (prefers sandy) soils, prairies

Range: eastern half of Colorado

Notes: Found growing in clumps, this true milkweed lacks milky sap; instead, its stem and leaves bleed clear sap. Species name *tuberosa* refers to its large taproot, which makes it nearly impossible to transplant. Can be grown from seed. Single stems branch only near the top and flower stalks harbor up to 25 individual flowers. Its roots and stems have been used in folk medicine. A host plant for Gray Hairstreak and Monarch caterpillars.

CLUSTER TYPE	FLOWER TYPE	LEAF TYPE	LEAF ATTACHMENT	FRUIT
Flat	Irregular	Simple	Alternate	Pod

SPREADING DOGBANE
Apocynum androsaemifolium

Family: Dogbane (Apocynaceae)

Height: 1-4' (30-120 cm)

Flower: pink to white, ⅓" (.8 cm) long, 5 petals fuse to form a tiny white bell with pink stripes inside; flowers in groups of 2-10

Leaf: oval, 2-4" (5-10 cm) long, toothless, often with a wavy edge

Fruit: long thin green pod, turning brown with age, 3-8" (7.5-20 cm) long; opens along 1 side, revealing seeds attached to long tufts of white fuzz

Bloom: summer

Cycle/Origin: perennial, native

Zone/Habitat: foothills, montane, subalpine; dry soils, along roads, woodland edges, sun

Range: western half of Colorado

Notes: A tall perennial with a single main stem that branches into many spreading stems. A close relative of milkweed, it produces a thick milky juice in its stems and leaves. This juice contains cardiac glycosides, which cause hot flashes, rapid heartbeat and fatigue. Insects avoid this plant because of the toxic juice. When dried and peeled, the stem makes a strong cord, which was once used by American Indians for fishing and trapping. The same fibers are selectively used by orioles as nest-building material.

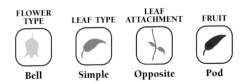

FLOWER TYPE	LEAF TYPE	LEAF ATTACHMENT	FRUIT
Bell	Simple	Opposite	Pod

MOSS CAMPION
Silene acaulis

Family: Pink (Caryophyllaceae)

Height: 2-3" (5-7.5 cm)

Flower: pink (rarely white), ½" (1 cm) wide, 5 notched petals; reddish green "bladder" (calyx), ⅜" (.9 cm) long, is behind the flower

Leaf: grass-like, ½-1½" (1-4 cm) long, basally attached; plants can form dense mats

Bloom: summer

Cycle/Origin: perennial, native

Zone/Habitat: alpine; rocky tundra

Range: western half of Colorado

Notes: Moss Campion flowers are a special sight for mountain hikers in Colorado, as the plants are slow to mature and may not bloom until they are 10 years old. Individual plants grow easily among rocks and in rock crevices, but can also form dense mats that produce an abundance of pink flowers. Mats can grow as wide as 1-2 feet (30-60 cm). Although it is native only in the alpine life zone, Moss Campion can be grown from seed at low elevations in rock gardens.

FLOWER TYPE	LEAF TYPE	LEAF ATTACHMENT
Regular	Simple	Basal

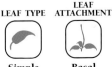

TWINFLOWER
Linnaea borealis

Family: Honeysuckle (Caprifoliaceae)

Height: 3-6" (7.5-15 cm)

Flower: pink, ½" (1 cm) long, with 5 petals fused to form a bell; flowers are in pairs and hang from a single thinly forked stem

Leaf: small and round, ½" (1 cm) wide, shiny light green, toothless; evergreen leaves are paired low on stem

Bloom: summer

Cycle/Origin: perennial, native

Zone/Habitat: montane, subalpine; conifer woods, bogs, rocky outcroppings

Range: western half of Colorado

Notes: A low-growing evergreen plant, Twinflower forms patches by trailing stems along the ground and sending up short thin flower stalks with a pair of leaves near the base and a pair or "twin" set of fragrant pink flowers. This common flower is found in northern conifer forests throughout the world (circumpolar). The genus name *Linnaea* honors the father of botany, Carolus Linnaeus, who developed the modern way of naming plants and animals by using two names–genus and species, usually of Latin, but sometimes Greek, derivation.

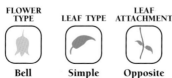

FLOWER TYPE	LEAF TYPE	LEAF ATTACHMENT
Bell	Simple	Opposite

CANADA THISTLE
Cirsium arvense

Family: Aster (Asteraceae)

Height: 1-5' (30-150 cm)

Flower: dark pink to light purple, ½-¾" (1-2 cm) wide, numerous flower parts enclosed by overlapping prickly green bracts with hooked tips; flower heads each on its own stem

Leaf: irregularly lobed, 5-8" (13-20 cm) long, each lobe ends in a sharp spine, light green with wavy edges and soft woolly hairs underneath, stalkless; lower leaves are larger and more lobed than upper; stems lack spines

Bloom: summer, fall

Cycle/Origin: perennial, non-native

Zone/Habitat: plains, foothills, montane; roadsides, old fields, barnyards, railways and other disturbed areas

Range: throughout

Notes: The most common and widespread thistle in Colorado. Also known as Corn Thistle because it often grows in cornfields. New plants are established by airborne seeds that can travel up to several miles. A non-native plant introduced to Canada (hence its common name) from France in the late 1700s, now considered a noxious weed. Many county governments have developed eradication plans to stop the spread of Canada Thistle.

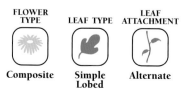

FLOWER TYPE	LEAF TYPE	LEAF ATTACHMENT
Composite	Simple Lobed	Alternate

FAIRY PRIMROSE
Primula angustifolia

Family: Primrose (Primulaceae)

Height: 2-4" (5-10 cm)

Flower: pink, ½-¾" (1-2 cm) wide, made up of 5 notched petals surrounding a light yellow center; petals are very delicate

Leaf: elongated, ½-2" (1-5 cm) long, fleshy, covered with fine hair, short leafstalk, basally attached

Bloom: summer

Cycle/Origin: perennial, native

Zone/Habitat: alpine; meadows, rocky soils, near melting snow

Range: western half of Colorado

Notes: Fairy Primrose grows abundantly in the high country of Colorado. Found growing in clumps, adding splashes of brilliant color to the tundra. Its short height is an adaptation to protect it from cold mountain winds. Although beautiful, the flowers give off a strong unpleasant odor, which attracts insect pollinators looking for carrion. Also known as Alpine Primrose.

FLOWER TYPE	LEAF TYPE	LEAF ATTACHMENT

Regular	Simple	Basal

PARRY PRIMROSE
Primula parryi

Family: Primrose (Primulaceae)

Height: 10-15" (25-38 cm)

Flower: deep pink, ½-1" (1-2.5 cm) long, made up of 5 delicate petals surrounding a yellow center; flowers arranged in groups at top of stems

Leaf: lance-shaped, 4-12" (10-30 cm) long, thick, basally attached

Bloom: summer

Cycle/Origin: perennial, native

Zone/Habitat: alpine; along streams, wet meadows, moist slopes

Range: western half of Colorado

Notes: Found in the high country of Colorado, Parry Primrose shares much of the same habitat as the closely related Fairy Primrose (pg. 65). Parry Primrose is taller than Fairy Primrose, making it easy to distinguish between the two. The flowers emit a carrion-like odor, but their beauty makes this wildflower a favorite of hikers. Plants in the Primrose family are not related to roses. "Primrose" in the common name is a misnomer and is actually a misinterpretation of a French word meaning "the first flower of spring," referring to its early blooming habit.

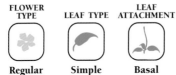

FLOWER TYPE	LEAF TYPE	LEAF ATTACHMENT
Regular	Simple	Basal

DWARF CLOVER
Trifolium nanum

Family: Pea or Bean (Fabaceae)

Height: 1-2" (2.5-5 cm)

Flower: 2-toned, pink with white or red, ¾" (2 cm) long, pea-like

Leaf: lance-shaped, ½-1" (1-2.5 cm) long, fleshy with a pointed tip, basally attached; leaves form mats

Bloom: summer

Cycle/Origin: perennial, native

Zone/Habitat: subalpine, alpine; mountain slopes, rocky tundra meadows

Range: western half of Colorado

Notes: A very common plant in the high country, thriving above the timberline. The flowers display their colors in midsummer and are a joy for Colorado hikers to behold. High velocity, desiccating winds do not harm a plant that is only a few inches tall. Dwarf Clover has adapted to its harsh habitat with its short height and thick leaves that retain moisture. Forms mats that can cover a large surface area in rocky tundra meadows. Like most clovers, Dwarf Clover flowers attract butterflies and bees.

FLOWER
TYPE

Irregular

LEAF TYPE

Simple

LEAF
ATTACHMENT

Basal

WESTERN MEADOW ASTER
Symphyotrichum campestre

Family: Aster (Asteraceae)

Height: 10-18" (25-45 cm)

Flower: pink to pale lavender, ¾" (2 cm) wide, with 15-30 petals (ray flowers) surrounding a small yellow center (disk flowers); downward-curved (recurved) green bracts; flowers found atop stems branching into many stalks

Leaf: lance-shaped, up to 1½" (4 cm) long, alternately attached

Bloom: summer, fall

Cycle/Origin: perennial, native

Zone/Habitat: foothills, montane, subalpine; forest openings, open hillsides, fields

Range: western half of Colorado

Notes: Also known as Field Aster, this small shrub-like plant has numerous stems that branch into many stalks. Can be confused with Colorado Tansy-aster (pg. 77) or Western Aster (pg. 139), but neither has the thin branching stems of Western Meadow Aster. Look for the recurved bracts beneath the composite flower heads to help identify. The bracts and stems are sticky. This plant spreads from horizontal underground stems (rhizomes). Western Meadow Aster blooms well into fall.

FLOWER TYPE

Composite

LEAF TYPE

Simple

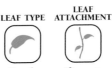

LEAF ATTACHMENT

Alternate

SHOOTING STAR
Dodecatheon pulchellum

Family: Primrose (Primulaceae)

Height: 10-20" (25-50 cm)

Flower: dark pink, 1" (2.5 cm) wide, 5 backward-curved petals and a pointed yellow center; each plant has only 1 stalk, which produces 1-5 nodding flowers

Leaf: lance-shaped, up to 6" (15 cm) long, round tip, toothless, basally attached

Bloom: spring, summer

Cycle/Origin: perennial, native

Zone/Habitat: foothills, montane, subalpine; dry soils, forests, sun or shade

Range: western half of Colorado

Notes: A common spring wildflower, Shooting Star was once called Prairie Pointers by early prairie settlers. The pointed center of each flower is composed of united stamens, an arrangement that makes insects force their tongues between the stamens to sip nectar. The flowers grow downward, but the flower stalk becomes upright after pollination. Often grown in gardens, the common name comes from its star-shaped flower that arches at the top of a long thin "shooting" stem.

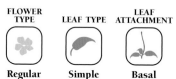

FLOWER TYPE	LEAF TYPE	LEAF ATTACHMENT
Regular	Simple	Basal

PINEYWOODS GERANIUM
Geranium caespitosum

Family: Geranium (Geraniaceae)

Height: 12-26" (30-66 cm)

Flower: pink to light purple, 1-1½" (2.5-4 cm) wide, 5 rounded petals with dark pink veins; flowers in loose groups on multi-branched stems

Leaf: lobed, 1-3" (2.5-7.5 cm) wide, 5-7 deep lobes, coarsely toothed, on long stalks, basally attached

Fruit: elongated triangular green seedpod, turning brown, 1-1½" (2.5-4 cm) long, hairy

Bloom: spring, summer

Cycle/Origin: perennial, native

Zone/Habitat: foothills, montane, subalpine; dry meadows, forest openings, hillsides

Range: western half of Colorado

Notes: There are about 800 species in the Geranium family occurring worldwide, 3 of which are found in Colorado. This species is one of the most common geraniums in the state. Pineywoods Geranium can be seen throughout the mountains, except in the alpine zone. Branching leafy stems have numerous flowers in spring and summer. The flowers have dark pink veins that reflect ultraviolet light, attracting many insects (especially bees). American Indians used geraniums to treat sores and to stop bleeding. Also known as Wild Geranium.

FLOWER TYPE
Regular

LEAF TYPE
Simple Lobed

LEAF ATTACHMENT
Basal

FRUIT
Pod

COLORADO TANSY-ASTER
Machaeranthera coloradoensis

Family: Aster (Asteraceae)

Height: 3-6" (7.5-15 cm)

Flower: pink to light purple, 1-1½" (2.5-4 cm) wide, made up of 15-30 petals (ray flowers) surrounding a yellowish center (disk flowers); green bracts at base of the flower are in 3 rows and have pointed tips

Leaf: elongated spoon-shaped, 2-3" (5-7.5 cm) long, hairy, toothed, alternately attached

Bloom: summer

Cycle/Origin: perennial, native

Zone/Habitat: montane, subalpine, alpine; rocky slopes, hillsides, forest openings

Range: western half of Colorado

Notes: Tansy-asters and asters are members of the same family, but are in different genera. They look similar at first glance, but close inspection of the bracts will help to identify a tansy-aster. Colorado Tansy-aster is much shorter than Bigelow Tansy-aster (pg. 127). It grows and blooms quickly due to the short summer growing season of high altitudes. Has a large woody taproot, in which it stores energy to survive the long Colorado winters. Spreads by horizontal underground stems (rhizomes). A food source for elk and deer that graze at high elevations.

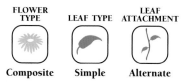

FLOWER TYPE	LEAF TYPE	LEAF ATTACHMENT
Composite	Simple	Alternate

FAIRY SLIPPER
Calypso bulbosa

Family: Orchid (Orchidaceae)

Height: 3-8" (7.5-20 cm)

Flower: mostly pink, 1-2" (2.5-5 cm) wide, made up of 3 petal-like sepals, 2 upper petals and 1 inflated lower petal (slipper); lower petal is white with reddish purple spots and stripes

Leaf: egg-shaped and flat, 1-2½" (2.5-4 cm) long, basally attached; 1 leaf per plant

Fruit: elliptical green capsule, turning brown with age, ¾" (2 cm) long; contains thousands of tiny seeds

Bloom: spring, early summer

Cycle/Origin: perennial, native

Zone/Habitat: foothills, montane, subalpine; wet areas in shady forests with moss mounds, near bogs and springs

Range: western half of Colorado

Notes: Also called Calypso Orchid, this plant is an endangered species. Even a slight tug when picking the flower will kill the plant, as the roots are extremely delicate. Rarely does well in gardens due to its strict soil requirements, and transplantation should not be attempted. Attracts insect pollinators (especially bees) with its fragrance. Flowers contain no nectar and pollen is inaccessible, thus bees receive no reward in exchange for pollination. However, the flowers continually change patterns, colors and even scent, so bees will visit other Fairy Slipper flowers even after a fruitless visit.

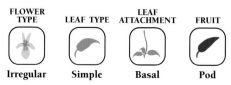

FLOWER TYPE	LEAF TYPE	LEAF ATTACHMENT	FRUIT
Irregular	Simple	Basal	Pod

ASPEN FLEABANE
Erigeron speciosus

Family: Aster (Asteraceae)

Height: 12-30" (30-76 cm)

Flower: light pink to light purple, 1-2" (2.5-5 cm) wide, composed of numerous thin petals (ray flowers) surrounding a yellow center (disk flowers)

Leaf: lance-shaped, 3-5" (7.5-13 cm) long, soft, smooth, basally and alternately attached

Bloom: summer

Cycle/Origin: perennial, native

Zone/Habitat: foothills, montane, subalpine; aspen groves, moist meadows, forest edges

Range: western half of Colorado

Notes: A common flower of the foothills and montane life zones in Colorado, Aspen Fleabane is sometimes confused with other flowers in the Aster family. Look for the numerous thin flower petals and the soft, lance-shaped leaves to help identify. The stems branch into stalks that each support one showy flower head. Species name *speciosus* means "pretty," referring to the flowers. Some American Indian tribes used crushed plants from the genus *Erigeron* to make a salve for treating wounds. A host plant for the Northern Checkerspot butterfly. Also known as Showy Daisy.

FLOWER TYPE	LEAF TYPE	LEAF ATTACHMENT	LEAF ATTACHMENT
Composite	Simple	Alternate	Basal

LEAFYBRACT ASTER
Symphyotrichum foliaceum

Family: Aster (Asteraceae)

Height: 18-30" (45-76 cm)

Flower: pinkish to lavender, 1-2" (2.5-5 cm) wide, made up of 15-50 overlapping petals (ray flowers) that surround a yellow center (disk flowers); shingle-like green bracts beneath flower head; several flowers sit atop ascending stalks that arise from leafy stems

Leaf: lance-shaped, 5-8" (13-20 cm) long, alternately attached; lower leaves are stalked, upper (cauline) leaves clasp the stem

Bloom: summer, fall

Cycle/Origin: perennial, native

Zone/Habitat: foothills, montane, subalpine; forest openings, moist places, along roads and ponds

Range: western half of Colorado

Notes: Leafybract Aster can easily be identified by its distinctive whorls of hairy curved bracts beneath each flower head and its hairy reddish stems. Also called Leafy Aster due to its many long leaves. Spreads from creeping horizontal underground stems and usually grows in clumps. Leafybract Asters growing in high elevations will be larger than those found in low altitudes. Wildlife such as deer and elk graze on the long leaves and stout stems.

FLOWER TYPE	LEAF TYPE	LEAF ATTACHMENT	LEAF ATTACHMENT
Composite	Simple	Alternate	Clasping

WILD ROSE
Rosa woodsii

Family: Rose (Rosaceae)

Height: 3-5' (90-150 cm); shrub

Flower: pink, 1½-2½" (4-6 cm) wide, 5 petals surrounding a group of yellow flower parts (stamens); flowers usually in groups of 2-4

Leaf: compound, divided into 5-9 leaflets; each leaflet, 1-1½" (2.5-4 cm) long, oval, toothed; leaves are alternately attached

Fruit: green berry-like fruit, turning slightly yellow, then red, ¼" (.6 cm) wide, hard, round; fruit is called a "hip" and persists on the shrub over the winter

Bloom: summer

Cycle/Origin: perennial, native

Zone/Habitat: all life zones except alpine; forest edges, along gravel roads, valleys, sunny hillsides

Range: throughout

Notes: The thorny branches and stems and round hips of Wild Rose distinguish it from Prickly Rose (pg. 87), which has bristly branches and stems and pear-shaped hips. The entire hip is edible, but usually only the outer covering is eaten, as the inside is hairy and can irritate the stomach. American Indians ate rose hips, mostly as emergency food. The fragrant flowers attract many insect pollinators. Known to hybridize with other species, which makes positive identification difficult. Also known as Wood Rose.

FLOWER TYPE	LEAF TYPE	LEAF ATTACHMENT	FRUIT
	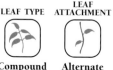		
Regular	Compound	Alternate	Berry

PRICKLY ROSE
Rosa acicularis

Family: Rose (Rosaceae)

Height: 2-4' (60-120 cm); shrub

Flower: bright pink, 2-2½" (5-6 cm) wide, composed of 5 delicate petals surrounding a group of yellow flower parts (stamens)

Leaf: compound, divided into 5-9 leaflets; each leaflet, 1-1½" (2.5-4 cm) long, teardrop-shaped, toothed, prominent veins; leaves are alternately attached

Fruit: green berry-like fruit, turning slightly yellow, then red, ½-¾" (1-2 cm) long, pear-shaped; fruit is called a "hip"

Bloom: summer

Cycle/Origin: perennial, native

Zone/Habitat: foothills, montane, subalpine; forest openings and edges, mountain slopes

Range: western half of Colorado

Notes: The stems and branches of this plant are covered with prickly bristles, hence "Prickly" in the common name. Spreads by underground roots, especially at forest edges and in rocky thickets, thereby forming large colonies. Similar appearance as Wild Rose (pg. 85), but has bristly branches and pear-shaped hips, compared to the thorny branches and round hips of Wild Rose. The red hips remain on the shrub during the winter, providing food for songbirds and wildlife. A host plant for the Striped Hairstreak butterfly.

FLOWER TYPE	LEAF TYPE	LEAF ATTACHMENT	FRUIT
Regular	Compound	Alternate	Berry

MUSK THISTLE
Carduus nutans

Family: Aster (Asteraceae)

Height: 3-6' (90-180 cm)

Flower: pink to light purple, 2-3" (5-7.5 cm) wide, made up of soft disk flowers only; flowers nod and have numerous sharp bracts

Leaf: lobed, 4-15" (10-38 cm) long, deep lobes, covered with spines and prickles, alternately attached; lower leaves are larger than upper

Bloom: summer, fall

Cycle/Origin: biennial, non-native

Zone/Habitat: plains, foothills, montane; disturbed areas, along roads, pastures, fields

Range: throughout

Notes: Musk Thistle was introduced from Europe and has spread rapidly throughout the West. Considered a noxious weed by the state of Colorado, efforts to reduce or eliminate it are being made. The large plants are very prickly; wear thick gloves if handling any part of this plant. The flowers attract insects, especially honeybees and bumblebees. Musk Thistle provides an emergency nectar source for hummingbirds. This plant is also called Bristle Thistle or Nodding Thistle.

FLOWER TYPE	LEAF TYPE	LEAF ATTACHMENT	LEAF ATTACHMENT
Composite	Simple Lobed	Alternate	Basal

GEYER ONION
Allium geyeri

Family: Lily (Liliaceae)

Height: 4-24" (10-60 cm)

Flower: tight round cluster, ½-1" (1-2.5 cm) wide, of tiny, light pink flowers; each flower, ¼" (.6 cm) wide, made up of overlapping pointed petals that form a tube that is narrow at the top

Leaf: long and grass-like, 4-24" (10-60 cm) long, basally attached; usually 3 leaves per stem

Bloom: summer

Cycle/Origin: perennial, native

Zone/Habitat: all life zones except plains; wet meadows, forest openings, hillsides

Range: western half of Colorado

Notes: Except in the plains, Geyer Onion grows in all life zones in Colorado. Those growing in the tundra habitat will be smaller, even dwarfed, compared to those found in the foothills. This plant has the typical oniony aroma, and both the leaves and bulbs are edible. American Indians harvested Geyer Onions throughout the summer and ate them raw and cooked. If harvesting bulbs for consumption, be sure to use the distinctive smell to distinguish between this plant and deadly species in the *Zigadenus* genus, such as Elegant Death Camas (pg. 263).

CLUSTER TYPE	FLOWER TYPE	LEAF TYPE	LEAF ATTACHMENT
Round	Tube	Simple	Basal

PINK PUSSYTOES
Antennaria rosea

Family: Aster (Asteraceae)

Height: 4-14" (10-36 cm)

Flower: round cluster, ½-2" (1-5 cm) wide, of tufts of light pink flowers; individual flower, ¼" (.6 cm) long, containing only disk flowers, usually white-tipped

Leaf: spoon-shaped, ¾" (2 cm) long, covered with fine whitish hairs; leaves are mainly basally attached

Bloom: spring, summer

Cycle/Origin: perennial, native

Zone/Habitat: foothills, montane, subalpine; in moist meadows, open woods, along streams

Range: western half of Colorado

Notes: This plant gets the latter part of its common name from the look and feel of the flower clusters, which resemble the pads of a cat's paw. Pink Pussytoes plants have either all male or all female flowers (dioecious), but both sexes appear similar. Sometimes reproduces without pollination, resulting in clones. Forms large mats in higher altitudes, where it spreads by sending out many runners. Genus name *Antennaria* means "antenna-like," referring to the rayless flowers. Also known as Rosy Pussytoes.

CLUSTER TYPE
Round

FLOWER TYPE
Composite

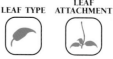
LEAF TYPE
Simple

LEAF ATTACHMENT
Basal

CHARMING WALLFLOWER
Erysimum capitatum purshii

Family: Mustard (Brassicaceae)

Height: 4-8" (10-20 cm)

Flower: round cluster, 1-2" (2.5-5 cm) wide, of bright pink flowers; each flower, ½-1" (1-2.5 cm) wide, has 4 round-to-oval petals surrounding a group of yellow flower parts (stamens)

Leaf: narrow, elongated, 1-5" (2.5-13 cm) long, tough, sometimes with toothed margins; basally attached leaves larger than alternately attached stem leaves

Fruit: thin green seedpod, turning brown with age, 2-4" (5-10 cm) long

Bloom: summer

Cycle/Origin: perennial, native

Zone/Habitat: subalpine, alpine; tundra slopes, alpine meadows, rocky ridges

Range: western half of Colorado

Notes: Charming Wallflower is a fragrant and showy plant of the high country. All wallflower species in Colorado are closely related—some botanists once considered them as one species with geographic variations. Now considered a variety of Alpine Wallflower (pg. 361), it grows in the same habitat as Alpine and has even been called by that common name. However, Charming Wallflower has pink flowers and is quite a bit smaller overall than Alpine Wallflower. Its flowers are pollinated by insects.

CLUSTER TYPE	FLOWER TYPE	LEAF TYPE	LEAF ATTACHMENT	LEAF ATTACHMENT	FRUIT
Round	Regular	Simple	Alternate	Basal	Pod

ROSY PAINTBRUSH
Castilleja rhexiifolia

Family: Snapdragon (Scrophulariaceae)

Height: 1-2' (30-60 cm)

Flower: tight spike cluster, 1-2½" (2.5-6 cm) long, made up of tiny green flowers hidden among pink (sometimes red or purple) bracts

Leaf: elongated oval, 1-2½" (2.5-6 cm) long, pointed tips, 3 veins, alternately attached

Fruit: pod-like green container, turning brown, ¾" (2 cm) long, contains seeds; container is hidden among dried-up bracts

Bloom: summer

Cycle/Origin: perennial, native

Zone/Habitat: alpine; meadows, hillsides

Range: western half of Colorado

Notes: At first glance, Rosy Paintbrush may be confused with Giant Red Paintbrush (pg. 179), but closer inspection will reveal the bracts of the latter are a distinctive bright scarlet red. Rosy Paintbrush has bracts that vary in color from pink to light red to purple. Most paintbrush species hybridize with each other, which further complicates identification. Found in high altitudes, hence it is also called Alpine Paintbrush (same common name, but not the Alpine Paintbrush on pg. 371). Also known as Splitleaf Indian Paintbrush. Paintbrush flowers provide nectar for hummingbirds, and some speculate that the two organisms co-evolved.

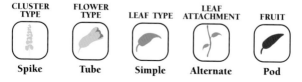

CLUSTER TYPE	FLOWER TYPE	LEAF TYPE	LEAF ATTACHMENT	FRUIT
Spike	Tube	Simple	Alternate	Pod

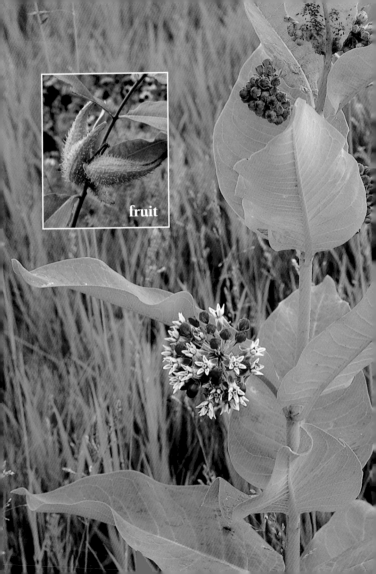

fruit

COMMON MILKWEED
Asclepias syriaca

Family: Milkweed (Asclepiadaceae)

Height: 2-5' (60-150 cm)

Flower: round cluster, 2-3" (5-7.5 cm) wide, made up of pink-tinged, cream-colored flowers; each flower, ½" (1 cm) wide, has 5 downward-pointing petals and a 5-part pointed crown

Leaf: oval, 4-6" (10-15 cm) long, large and toothless; bleeds a milky sap when broken

Fruit: elongated green pod, turning tan, 3-5" (7.5-13 cm) long; opens to release flat brown seeds; each seed attached to hair-like fuzz that becomes airborne

Bloom: spring, summer

Cycle/Origin: perennial, native

Zone/Habitat: plains, foothills, montane; wet or dry soils, fields

Range: throughout

Notes: There are over 2,000 milkweed species worldwide, 6 in Colorado. A unique pollination system involves sacs of pollen that snag on an insect's leg; the insect then unwittingly inserts the sacs into slits on other flowers. The plant's milky sap contains cardiac glycosides and, if eaten, will cause hot flashes, rapid heart rate and general weakness. The Monarch butterfly lays its eggs exclusively on milkweeds. Monarch caterpillars ingest the toxic sap with no ill effects, but they then become toxic to birds and other animals. Orioles use fibers from old milkweed stems to build nests.

CLUSTER TYPE	FLOWER TYPE	LEAF TYPE	LEAF ATTACHMENT	FRUIT
Round	Irregular	Simple	Opposite	Pod

ROCKY MOUNTAIN BEE PLANT
Cleome serrulata

Family: Caper (Capparaceae)

Height: 1-4' (30-120 cm)

Flower: round cluster, 2-4" (5-10 cm) wide, of pink to purple flowers; each flower, ½" (1 cm) wide, has 4 petals fused together at the base and 6 long yellow-tipped flower parts (stamens) extending beyond the petals

Leaf: palmate, divided into 3 leaflets, 1-3" (2.5-7.5 cm) long; leaves are alternately attached

Fruit: bean-like green seedpod, 2-3" (5-7.5 cm) long, dangles from a long arched stem that is jointed in the middle; seedpod stays green well into autumn

Bloom: summer

Cycle/Origin: annual, native

Zone/Habitat: plains, foothills, montane; sandy meadows, fields, along roads

Range: throughout

Notes: Rocky Mountain Bee Plant gives off a strong odor and is sometimes called Stinkweed or Stinking Clover. Bees are highly attracted to this plant despite the smell, hence "Bee" in the common name. Six yellow-tipped stamens extend beyond the pink petals, looking like pins in a pincushion. The leaves and seeds are edible, but have an unpleasant taste. American Indians considered this plant to be an important source of emergency food.

CLUSTER TYPE	FLOWER TYPE	LEAF TYPE	LEAF ATTACHMENT	FRUIT
Round	Tube	Palmate	Alternate	Pod

DOTTED BLAZING STAR
Liatris punctata

Family: Aster (Asteraceae)

Height: 6-24" (15-60 cm)

Flower: spike cluster, 2-5" (5-13 cm) long, of pink flowers crowded at top of the stem; tiny individual flower, made up of 4-8 disk flowers only, with protruding thread-like flower parts that look feathery

Leaf: thin, 2-6" (5-15 cm) long, stiff and sandpapery to the touch, alternately attached

Bloom: late summer, fall

Cycle/Origin: perennial, native

Zone/Habitat: plains, foothills; fields, dry slopes, open hillsides, along roads

Range: eastern half of Colorado

Notes: A common wildflower in fields of Colorado's plains and foothills. Blooms late in the growing season after many other plants have dried up. Dotted Blazing Star gets part of its common name from tiny resin dots on the leaves, which may or may not be visible. Used in a variety of ways by Plains Indians. Some tribes used it for a tea; others used it to soothe sore throats or mixed the mashed roots with honey for a cough syrup. Also known as Gayfeather.

CLUSTER TYPE	FLOWER TYPE	LEAF TYPE	LEAF ATTACHMENT
Spike	**Composite**	**Simple**	**Alternate**

ELEPHANT'S HEAD
Pedicularis groenlandica

Family: Snapdragon (Scrophulariaceae)

Height: 12-28" (30-71 cm)

Flower: spike cluster, 2-6" (5-15 cm) long, of dark pink-to-purple flowers; individual flower, ¾" (2 cm) long, has 2 petals (lips); each flower resembles the head of an elephant (see inset), with the upper lip forming the trunk and the lower lip forming the ears

Leaf: fern-like, 3-8" (7.5-20 cm) long, numerous lobes, basally and alternately attached

Bloom: summer

Cycle/Origin: perennial, native

Zone/Habitat: montane, subalpine, alpine; wet meadows, along streams, seeps and ponds

Range: western half of Colorado

Notes: In wet summers, Elephant's Head will sometimes bloom in profusion, coloring entire meadows pink or purple. Aptly named, it does not take much imagination to see that each flower resembles the head, trunk and ears of an elephant in miniature (see inset). The complex structure of the flower makes pollination species specific, reducing any chance of hybridization. In addition, only specific bee species pollinate the flowers. Species name *groenlandica* refers to Greenland, the country in which this species was first identified.

CLUSTER TYPE	FLOWER TYPE	LEAF TYPE	LEAF ATTACHMENT	LEAF ATTACHMENT
Spike	Irregular	Simple Lobed	Alternate	Basal

PURPLE LOCOWEED
Oxytropis lambertii

Family: Pea or Bean (Fabaceae)

Height: 6-16" (15-40 cm)

Flower: spike cluster, 2-6" (5-15 cm) long, of pea-like, dark pink-to-purple flowers; each flower, ½-1" (1-2.5 cm) long; cluster on a leafless stem

Leaf: compound, 4-12" (10-30 cm) long; each leaflet, ½-1½" (1-4 cm) long, lance-shaped; leaves are basally attached; tiny hairs give leaf a silvery appearance

Fruit: ovate green pod, turning brown with age, ¼-½" (.6-1 cm) long

Bloom: spring, summer

Cycle/Origin: perennial, native

Zone/Habitat: all life zones except alpine; sandy soils, in forest openings, along roads

Range: throughout

Notes: There are several species of locoweeds in Colorado, all of them toxic to livestock and not well liked by ranchers. Toxicity level depends on the amount of the element selenium in the soil, and large amounts of the plant must be consumed to be lethal. Purple Locoweed is one of the most common springtime locoweeds of lower elevations. Sometimes covers large areas in colorful displays. An important nectar source for Broad-tailed Hummingbirds. Also known as Colorado Loco.

CLUSTER TYPE	FLOWER TYPE	LEAF TYPE	LEAF ATTACHMENT	FRUIT
Spike	Irregular	Compound	Basal	Pod

FIREWEED
Chamerion angustifolium

Family: Evening-primrose (Onagraceae)

Height: 2-6' (60-180 cm)

Flower: spike cluster, 6-12" (15-30 cm) long, with multiple pink flowers; individual flower, 1" (2.5 cm) wide, made up of 4 oval petals; flowers open individually from the bottom of the spike up

Leaf: narrow, willow-like, up to 8" (20 cm) long, finely toothed, alternately attached

Fruit: slender pod-like green container, turning tan, up to 3" (7.5 cm) long, opens from the top down to release silky down that carries the seeds away on the wind

Bloom: summer, fall

Cycle/Origin: perennial, native

Zone/Habitat: foothills, montane, subalpine; dry soils, along roads, recently burned woodlands, shade

Range: western half of Colorado

Notes: Fireweed is one of the first plants to grow after a forest fire, hence its common name. It grows in large masses after the wind has dispersed its seeds into burned areas, or individually in disturbed soils. A very common wildflower found in the western half of Colorado. Also known as Willow Herb because of its willow-shaped leaves. A good nectar source for many butterfly species.

CLUSTER TYPE	FLOWER TYPE	LEAF TYPE	LEAF ATTACHMENT	FRUIT
Spike	Regular	Simple	Alternate	Pod

MOUNTAIN BLUE VIOLET
Viola adunca

Family: Violet (Violaceae)

Height: 4-8" (10-20 cm)

Flower: purple to dark blue, ¾" (2 cm) long, composed of 2 backward-curved upper petals and 3 lower petals; hairy throat is white with purple stripes

Leaf: heart-shaped or oval, 1-2" (2.5-5 cm) long, stalked, alternately attached

Bloom: spring, summer

Cycle/Origin: perennial, native

Zone/Habitat: all life zones except plains; aspen groves, moist meadows, field edges

Range: western half of Colorado

Notes: Mountain Blue Violet is a common plant that grows in all mountainous habitats. However, because of its low ground-hugging growing habit, visitors to the high country often miss this beautiful plant. In addition, plants of the alpine zone will be smaller than those of lower elevations, so it is even easier to overlook this plant in higher altitudes. The seeds contain oil that attracts ants, which carry the seeds to their nests, thus dispersing Mountain Blue Violet to new areas. Also known as Hooked Spur Violet.

FLOWER TYPE

Irregular

LEAF TYPE

Simple

LEAF ATTACHMENT

Alternate

ALPINE COLUMBINE
Aquilegia saximontana

Family: Buttercup (Ranunculaceae)

Height: 4-8" (10-20 cm)

Flower: purple to dark blue, ¾" (2 cm) long, bell-shaped, composed of 5 white-tipped petals and 5 purple petal-like sepals that are lance-shaped; flowers nod at end of flower stalks

Leaf: compound, divided into as many as 5 leaflets; each leaflet, ⅜-1⅜" (1-3 cm) long, has 3 lobes

Fruit: elongated hairy green pod, turning brown with age, ¾" (2 cm) long

Bloom: summer

Cycle/Origin: perennial, native

Zone/Habitat: subalpine, alpine; rocky slopes

Range: western half of Colorado

Notes: Columbines are somewhat poisonous, thus American Indians sometimes used crushed seeds of Alpine Columbine to rid their hair of lice. The nectar-filled spurs can only be reached by the long tongues of hummingbirds and some species of moths. Genus name is from the Latin word *aquila* for "eagle," and refers to the shape of the flowers, which resemble eagle talons. The species name *saximontana* means "of the mountains."

FLOWER TYPE	LEAF TYPE	LEAF ATTACHMENT	FRUIT
Bell	Compound	Basal	Pod

HAREBELL
Campanula rotundifolia

Family: Bellflower (Campanulaceae)

Height: 6-20" (15-50 cm)

Flower: purple to blue, ¾" (2 cm) long, 5 petals are fused together to form a bell; found singly or in clusters nodding from a thin stem

Leaf: round, ½-1" (1-2.5 cm) wide, basally attached, often withering before flowering; upper is narrow and grass-like, 3" (7.5 cm) long and ⅛-¼" (.3-.6 cm) wide, alternately attached along the stem

Bloom: summer, fall

Cycle/Origin: perennial, native

Zone/Habitat: all life zones except plains; wet soils, rocky outcroppings along rivers, prairies, meadows, sun

Range: western half of Colorado

Notes: Harebell, one of four species of *Campanula* found in Colorado, is the smallest member with the thinnest and weakest stem. Its basal leaves are round, hence the species name, *rotundifolia*, or "round leaf." Like other members of this genus, its stems exude a milky sap. The drooping flowers are adapted for pollination by larger insects that are strong enough to cling to the flowers and also protect the pollen from rain and dew. Harebell often grows in clumps and does well in gardens, but please don't dig it from the wild. Also called Bluebell, this circumpolar plant grows at similar latitudes all around the world.

FLOWER TYPE	LEAF TYPE	LEAF ATTACHMENT	LEAF ATTACHMENT
Bell	Simple	Alternate	Basal

COMMON BURDOCK
Arctium minus

Family: Aster (Asteraceae)

Height: 2-6' (60-180 cm)

Flower: deep purplish, ¾-1" (2-2.5 cm) wide, composed of overlapping prickly green bracts with hooked tips that enclose numerous flower parts

Leaf: large and oval, up to 20" (50 cm) long; sometimes with heart-shaped lower leaves that are dark green and woolly beneath; hollow leafstalk

Bloom: summer, fall

Cycle/Origin: biennial, non-native

Zone/Habitat: plains, foothills; roadsides, near streams, old fields, barnyards, railways and other disturbed areas

Range: eastern half of Colorado

Notes: The large leaves and deep purple flowers make this plant hard to misidentify. Resembles the garden variety of rhubarb. After the flowers have been pollinated (usually by large bees), the seeds develop in prickly brown seed heads that easily catch on fur or clothing, thus providing an excellent seed dispersal mechanism. Seed heads are sometimes called nature's Velcro.

FLOWER TYPE	LEAF TYPE	LEAF ATTACHMENT	LEAF ATTACHMENT
Composite	Simple	Alternate	Basal

SPOTTED KNAPWEED
Centaurea stoebe

Family: Aster (Asteraceae)

Height: 2-3' (60-90 cm)

Flower: lavender to purple, 1" (2.5 cm) wide, made entirely of disk flowers surrounded underneath by a black-tipped, prickly brown bract; each plant produces 25-100 flower heads

Leaf: deeply lobed lower, 4-8" (10-20 cm) long, with many narrow lobes; much smaller upper, 1-2" (2.5-5 cm) long, also deeply lobed, with very narrow pointed lobes

Bloom: summer, fall

Cycle/Origin: annual or biennial, non-native

Zone/Habitat: plains, foothills; dry soils, open fields, along roads

Range: eastern half of Colorado

Notes: Spotted Knapweed is a non-native plant commonly found growing in large groups along roadsides and in open fields. It looks a lot like the garden annual, Bachelor Button (not shown). Its lavender flowers can range from white to red, but always have the triangular brown bracts. Its leaves often appear wilted and curled. Considered a noxious weed by many state agricultural departments due to its aggressiveness in crowding out other plants. Possibly an allelopathic plant that chemically changes soil to discourage other plants and favor its own new growth.

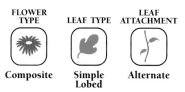

FLOWER TYPE	LEAF TYPE	LEAF ATTACHMENT
Composite	Simple Lobed	Alternate

SMOOTH BLUE ASTER
Symphyotrichum laeve

Family: Aster (Asteraceae)

Height: 1-3' (30-90 cm)

Flower: lavender to light blue, 1" (2.5 cm) wide, made up of 15-50 petals (ray flowers) surrounding a yellow center (disk flowers); plant has numerous flowers atop stems branching from a stout stalk

Leaf: lance-shaped, 4-6" (10-15 cm) long, hairless and thick, alternately attached; upper (cauline) clasps the stem

Bloom: summer, fall

Cycle/Origin: perennial, native

Zone/Habitat: plains, foothills, montane; open sites, meadows, hillsides

Range: throughout

Notes: Smooth Blue Aster provides color late in the growing season in Colorado, often blooming well into autumn. It provides nectar for butterflies and bees well after many other flowers have withered. "Smooth" in the common name refers to the texture of the hairless leaves and stems, and "Blue" is for its flower color (although it is usually lavender). Each stout tall stalk branches and gives rise to numerous flower heads. Spreads by horizontal underground stems (rhizomes). A yellow-to-orange dye can be made from the foliage.

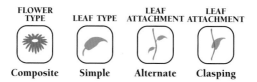

FLOWER TYPE	LEAF TYPE	LEAF ATTACHMENT	LEAF ATTACHMENT
Composite	Simple	Alternate	Clasping

FEATHERLEAF FLEABANE
Erigeron pinnatisectus

Family: Aster (Asteraceae)

Height: 4-5" (10-13 cm)

Flower: lavender, 1" (2.5 cm) wide, made up of delicate petals (ray flowers) surrounding a yellow center (disk flowers); hairy bracts at base of flower

Leaf: fern-like, 2-3" (5-7.5 cm) long, finely divided into lobes, basally attached

Bloom: summer

Cycle/Origin: perennial, native

Zone/Habitat: subalpine, alpine; rocky ridges, tundra slopes

Range: western half of Colorado

Notes: A plant of the high country, Featherleaf Fleabane has a short, but dramatic growing cycle. When the snow banks have melted, sprouts from cracks in rocks and in boulder fields and quickly produces blooms. The fern-like leaves and ray flowers are delicate and soft to the touch. Genus name *Erigeron* is from the Greek words for "early" and "old man," referring to the fluffy white seed heads that resemble the hair of an elderly gentleman. Seed heads appear soon after insects pollinate the flowers.

FLOWER TYPE	LEAF TYPE	LEAF ATTACHMENT
Composite	Simple Lobed	Basal

THREE-NERVE FLEABANE
Erigeron subtrinervis

Family: Aster (Asteraceae)

Height: 12-32" (30-80 cm)

Flower: light purple, 1-1½" (2.5-4 cm) wide, made up of as many as 100 thin petals (ray flowers) surrounding a bright yellow center (disk flowers)

Leaf: lance-shaped, 1-4" (2.5-10 cm) long, hairy, 3 prominent veins, alternately attached, slightly clasping a hairy stem; stems are multi-branched

Bloom: summer

Cycle/Origin: perennial, native

Zone/Habitat: foothills, montane, subalpine; meadows, forest openings, hillsides

Range: western half of Colorado

Notes: This Fleabane can be distinguished from other plants in the genus *Erigeron* by the hairy leaves with three well-defined veins or "nerves" and the hairy stems. In favorable growing conditions, Three-nerve Fleabane will grow tall and the stem will branch many times, giving rise to many showy flowers. Some American Indian tribes used a poultice of fleabane leaves mixed with animal fat to treat swollen or painful areas of the skin.

FLOWER TYPE	LEAF TYPE	LEAF ATTACHMENT	LEAF ATTACHMENT

Composite	**Simple**	**Alternate**	**Clasping**

BIGELOW TANSY-ASTER
Machaeranthera bigelovii

Family: Aster (Asteraceae)

Height: 2-4' (60-120 cm)

Flower: bright purple, 1-1½" (2.5-4 cm) wide, numerous thin petals (ray flowers) surrounding a yellow center (disk flowers); sticky green bracts at the base of the flower have recurved purplish tips

Leaf: lance-shaped, up to 6" (15 cm) long, coarsely toothed, alternately attached

Bloom: late summer, fall

Cycle/Origin: biennial, native

Zone/Habitat: foothills, montane; roadsides, along trails

Range: western half of Colorado

Notes: The sticky stem of Bigelow Tansy-aster branches numerous times, supporting many showy purple flowers. The petals fold up in the evening into a "sleep" position and open with the morning sunlight. Its leaves have a strong odor. Grows well in disturbed soils. Genus name *Machaeranthera* comes from the Greek *machaer* for "sword" and *anthos* for "flower," and refers to the shape of the male flower parts (anthers). Species name *bigelovii* honors botanist John Bigelow.

FLOWER TYPE	LEAF TYPE	LEAF ATTACHMENT	LEAF ATTACHMENT
Composite	Simple	Alternate	Basal

STICKY PURPLE GERANIUM
Geranium viscosissimum

Family: Geranium (Geraniaceae)

Height: 1-3' (30-90 cm)

Flower: light purple to dark pink, 1-1½" (2.5-4 cm) wide, 5 rounded petals with deep purple or dark green veins; flowers in groups on branching sticky stems

Leaf: lobed, 2-4" (5-10 cm) wide, 5-7 deep lobes with sharp teeth, on a long stalk, basally attached

Fruit: long thin green capsule, turning brown, 1-1½" (2.5-4 cm) long; capsule is hairy

Bloom: spring, summer

Cycle/Origin: perennial, native

Zone/Habitat: foothills, montane; forest openings, meadows, along roads

Range: western half of Colorado

Notes: Sticky Purple Geranium is so named because of its sticky stem, which is covered with glandular hairs. Has many leafy branched stems, and the purple or pink flowers are heavily veined in deep purple or dark green. Grows in clumps. Geraniums do hybridize, so look closely for minute differences to help identify. Inspect the underside of the leaves–only the veins have hairs in this species. The genus name *Geranium* is from the Greek *geranos*, meaning "crane." Also known as Western Crane's Bill, named for the shape of the seed capsule, which resembles the bill of a crane.

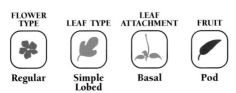

FLOWER TYPE	LEAF TYPE	LEAF ATTACHMENT	FRUIT
Regular	Simple Lobed	Basal	Pod

BRITTON SKULLCAP
Scutellaria brittonii

Family: Mint (Lamiaceae)

Height: 4-8" (10-20 cm)

Flower: purple to dark blue, 1-1½" (2.5-4 cm) long, trumpet-shaped, composed of 2 petals (lips) fused to form a tube, wider lower lip is flared and has a white stripe; flowers found in pairs

Leaf: oblong, 1-3" (2.5-7.5 cm) long, hairy, oppositely attached

Bloom: spring, early summer

Cycle/Origin: perennial, native

Zone/Habitat: plains, foothills, montane; dry open slopes, forest openings, gravelly areas among pines

Range: throughout

Notes: Britton Skullcap is a pretty wildflower usually seen growing in small groups, with one pair (sometimes more) of flowers per stem. This small member of the Mint family blooms early, displaying purple color for early season hikers to enjoy. The flowers are unmistakable with their large lower and smaller upper lips. This plant contains antispasmodic compounds that were once used to treat some nervous conditions. The first part of the common name and the species name *brittonii* honor American botanist Nathaniel Lord Britton.

FLOWER TYPE	LEAF TYPE	LEAF ATTACHMENT
Irregular	**Simple**	**Opposite**

HAIRY CLEMATIS
Clematis hirsutissima

Family: Buttercup (Ranunculaceae)

Height: 12-30" (30-76 cm)

Flower: dark purple, 1-2" (2.5-5 cm) long, bell-shaped, made up of 4 petal-like sepals and yellow flower parts (stamens)

Leaf: twice compound, finely divided into many leaflets; each leaflet, 2-5" (5-13 cm) long, hairy

Bloom: spring, summer

Cycle/Origin: perennial, native

Zone/Habitat: plains, foothills, montane; meadows, openings in forests, prairies

Range: throughout

Notes: Hairy Clematis is known by numerous other common names such as Sugarbowls, Leather Flower or Vase Flower. Most other clematis plants are vines; Hairy Clematis is not–it grows in bushy clumps that contain several stems. A single deep purple or dull reddish flower hangs from the top of each stem and looks like an inverted urn. Prefers open habitat and will not grow well in the shade. Insects (especially bees) are its chief pollinators.

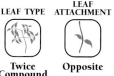

FLOWER TYPE	LEAF TYPE	LEAF ATTACHMENT
Bell	Twice Compound	Opposite

MOUNTAIN GENTIAN
Gentiana parryi

Family: Gentian (Gentianaceae)

Height: 4-14" (10-36 cm)

Flower: purple, 1-2" (2.5-5 cm) long, goblet-shaped, with 5 petals fused to 5 petal-like sepals; sometimes the outside of tube has green stripes

Leaf: broadly oval, ½-1½" (1-4 cm) long, thick, pointed, oppositely attached

Bloom: summer, early fall

Cycle/Origin: perennial, native

Zone/Habitat: montane, subalpine; in moist meadows, along streams, bogs

Range: western half of Colorado

Notes: Mountain Gentian appears similar to other gentians, but is a particularly leafy species, with branching stems that sometimes give rise to as many as three flowers. Look for the large smooth leaves and the showy purple flowers to help identify. Although more common than other gentians in Colorado, this plant might be overlooked on cloudy days, as the flowers only open when it is sunny. The purple color of the flowers attracts bees and other insect pollinators. Gentians have some medicinal properties such as appetite stimulation for people with prolonged illnesses. Also known as Parry Gentian.

FLOWER TYPE

Tube

LEAF TYPE

Simple

LEAF ATTACHMENT

Opposite

ROCKY MOUNTAIN FRINGED GENTIAN
Gentianopsis thermalis

Family: Gentian (Gentianaceae)

Height: 6-15" (15-38 cm)

Flower: dark purple with a white inside, 1½-2½" (4-6 cm) long, delicate petals fringed at the ends; 4 petal-like green sepals with pointed ends surround the petals at the base

Leaf: lance-shaped, 1-2" (2.5-5 cm) long, smooth and oppositely attached

Bloom: summer

Cycle/Origin: annual, native

Zone/Habitat: montane, subalpine; wet meadows, along streams

Range: western half of Colorado

Notes: Rocky Mountain Fringed Gentian is usually found growing in clumps, and groups of the showy purple flowers are a delight to see. Look for it near high mountain springs and seeps in Colorado. Species name *thermalis* means "of warmth," referring to the habitat of the Yellowstone National Park area, where it grows in profusion near geyser basins and hot springs. The species has several varieties that differ slightly from each other, depending upon the region in which each grows. "Gentian" in the common name is derived from Gentius, king of ancient Illyria, who discovered the medicinal properties of the plants.

FLOWER TYPE	LEAF TYPE	LEAF ATTACHMENT
Tube	Simple	Opposite

WESTERN ASTER
Symphyotrichum ascendens

Family: Aster (Asteraceae)

Height: 8-24" (20-60 cm)

Flower: pale lavender, 2" (5 cm) wide, with 15-50 petals (ray flowers) surrounding a yellow center (disk flowers); bristly green bracts are in 3 or 4 overlapping rows at the base of the flower head

Leaf: grass-like, up to 6" (15 cm) long, alternate attachment; lower leaves are stalked, upper (cauline) clasp the reddish stems, both types are toothless

Bloom: summer, fall

Cycle/Origin: perennial, native

Zone/Habitat: foothills, montane, subalpine; rocky hillsides, slopes, near ponds and marshes, along roads

Range: western half of Colorado

Notes: Western Aster grows abundantly in Colorado. Spreads by horizontal underground stems (rhizomes) and, as a result, is seen growing in clumps. Bristly bracts at the bases of the flowers are arranged in three or four overlapping rows. The flower stems are wiry and sticky to the touch. Look for the reddish leafstalks and the long, grass-like leaves to help identify. Also called Purple Aster, the flowers attract bees and butterflies.

FLOWER TYPE	LEAF TYPE	LEAF ATTACHMENT	LEAF ATTACHMENT
Composite	Simple	Alternate	Clasping

ROCKY MOUNTAIN IRIS
Iris missouriensis

Family: Iris (Iridaceae)

Height: 8-20" (20-50 cm)

Flower: purple to light blue, 2-3½" (5-9 cm) wide, made up of 3 upright petals and 3 backward-curving, petal-like sepals with yellow streaks

Leaf: narrow, sword-like, 6-20" (15-50 cm) long, thick and flexible, basally attached

Fruit: large 3-parted green pod, turning brown with age, 1½-2" (4-5 cm) long

Bloom: spring, summer

Cycle/Origin: perennial, native

Zone/Habitat: foothills, montane, subalpine; wet meadows, along streams, seeps and roads

Range: western half of Colorado

Notes: Rocky Mountain Iris flowers, which resemble those of cultivated irises, are exceptionally intricate and beautiful. Plants will form large dense clumps in a habitat with sufficient moisture. Although this plant has some reported medicinal uses, the roots are poisonous and should never be eaten. Many American Indian tribes mixed the roots with bile to use as a poison on arrow tips. *Iris* is Greek for "rainbow," referring to the many colors of flowers in the genus. Also known as Mountain Iris or Snake Iris, the latter name referring to the leaves, which are shaped like a serpent.

FLOWER TYPE	LEAF TYPE	LEAF ATTACHMENT	FRUIT
Irregular	Simple	Basal	Pod

SKY PILOT
Polemonium viscosum

Family: Phlox (Polemoniaceae)

Height: 4-14" (10-36 cm)

Flower: loose round cluster, 1-2" (2.5-5 cm) wide, of light purple or lavender-to-sky blue flowers; individual tubular flower, ½-1" (1-2.5 cm) long, has 5 lobes surrounding a group of pollen-covered yellow flower parts (stamens)

Leaf: compound, 4-6" (10-15 cm) long, divided into many leaflets; each leaflet, ½" (1 cm) long, hairy and odorous; leaves are basally attached

Bloom: summer

Cycle/Origin: perennial, native

Zone/Habitat: alpine; rocky ridges, tundra slopes, along trails

Range: western half of Colorado

Notes: Sky Pilot is beautiful in bloom, adding lots of color to the tundra habitat of Colorado. Flourishes along man-made trails and alpine meadows dug up by gophers or ground squirrels. Its leaves emit a strong odor, earning another common name, Skunkweed. Sometimes hiker's boots will reek of the offensive odor after walking through high country meadows containing Sky Pilot. The tubular flowers reflect ultraviolet light, which attracts insects. This plant is also known as Sticky Polemonium.

CLUSTER TYPE	FLOWER TYPE	LEAF TYPE	LEAF ATTACHMENT

Round	**Tube**	**Compound**	**Basal**

ALFALFA
Medicago sativa

Family: Pea or Bean (Fabaceae)

Height: 1-3' (30-90 cm)

Flower: tight spike cluster, 1-2" (2.5-5 cm) long, of deep purple-to-dark blue flowers (can range to light blue); each flower, ¼-⅓" (.6-.8 cm) long, with 1 large upper petal and 3 smaller lower petals

Leaf: 3-parted and clover-like, 1-2" (2.5-5 cm) long

Fruit: green seedpod, turning nearly black with age; twists into coils

Bloom: spring, summer, fall

Cycle/Origin: perennial, non-native

Zone/Habitat: plains, foothills; dry soils, fields, along roads, sun

Range: eastern half of Colorado

Notes: This deep-rooted perennial is usually found along roads or fields where it has escaped cultivation. Alfalfa is often planted by farmers as a food crop for farm animals and to improve soil fertility by fixing nitrogen from air into the soil through its roots. A winter-hardy variety of alfalfa developed in the late 1800s was partially responsible for the establishment of the dairy industry in the upper Midwest in the early 1900s. The thin stems often cause the plant to fall over under its own weight when mature, leaving it prostrate. Flower color can range from dark purple to light blue. A prime host plant for the alfalfa butterfly, Orange Sulphur.

CLUSTER TYPE	FLOWER TYPE	LEAF TYPE	LEAF ATTACHMENT	FRUIT
Spike	Irregular	Compound	Alternate	Pod

COMMON GRAPE HYACINTH
Muscari botryoides

Family: Lily (Liliaceae)

Height: 8-12" (20-30 cm)

Flower: spike cluster, 2-3" (5-7.5 cm) long, of purple-to-dark blue flowers; individual flower, ¼" (.6 cm) long, round to oval, hanging down; flowers are clustered at the end of a single stalk

Leaf: grass-like, 6-12" (15-30 cm) long, basally attached; 2 or 3 leaves per plant; leaves arch in an inverted U shape

Bloom: spring

Cycle/Origin: perennial, non-native

Zone/Habitat: plains, foothills; fields, meadows, along roads

Range: eastern half of Colorado

Notes: Common Grape Hyacinth is one of the first plants to sprout and bloom in eastern Colorado. Will emerge as soon as the snow melts in spring, and because it blooms so early, often is blanketed by late spring snowstorms. Flowers have both male and female plant parts (hermaphroditic). Insects such as flies or beetles, but especially bees, pollinate the flowers. The flowers are edible to humans, but only after being pickled; ground squirrels, rabbits and deer eat the fresh blooms. Easy to grow in home gardens, this plant has escaped from cultivation and now also grows in the wild. The cultivated flower clusters are very popular in flower arrangements.

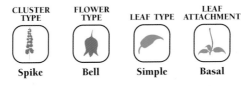

CLUSTER TYPE	FLOWER TYPE	LEAF TYPE	LEAF ATTACHMENT
Spike	Bell	Simple	Basal

TWO-LOBE LARKSPUR
Delphinium nuttallianum

Family: Buttercup (Ranunculaceae)

Height: 8-12" (20-30 cm)

Flower: loose spike cluster, 2-4" (5-10 cm) long, of purple-to-dark blue flowers; each flower, ½-1" (1-2.5 cm) long, composed of 5 petal-like sepals and 4 purple petals; upper sepal forms spur, ½-¾" (1-2 cm) long

Leaf: lobed, ¾-2" (2-5 cm) wide, deeply divided into thin finger-like lobes, stalked, alternately attached

Fruit: hairy green seedpod, turning brown, ½" (1 cm) long

Bloom: spring

Cycle/Origin: perennial, native

Zone/Habitat: plains, foothills, montane; dry slopes, open areas, forest openings

Range: throughout

Notes: Two-lobe Larkspur is sometimes known as Early Larkspur because it is one of the first spring flowers to bloom. In favorable dry growing conditions, Colorado hillsides are splashed with purple color. Spreads by sending out tuber-like roots. Most parts of this plant contain poisonous alkaloids and should never be eaten or touched by humans. Ingesting large amounts can be fatal and ranchers have reported losing cattle as a result. Pollen and dried petals were used by Navajo Indians in religious ceremonies and to treat infestations of lice.

CLUSTER TYPE	FLOWER TYPE	LEAF TYPE	LEAF ATTACHMENT	FRUIT
Spike	Irregular	Simple Lobed	Alternate	Pod

MONKSHOOD
Aconitum columbianum

Family: Buttercup (Ranunculaceae)

Height: 2-6' (60-180 cm)

Flower: loose spike cluster, 2-6" (5-15 cm) long, of deep purple (very rarely white) flowers; each flower, 1¼-1½" (3-4 cm) long, made of 5 petal-like sepals, the uppermost forming a "hood," ¼-1¼" (.6-3 cm) long, that covers the other flower parts

Leaf: lobed, 2-8" (5-20 cm) wide, deeply cut into 3-5 lobes; each lobe is toothed; lower leaves on long stalks, upper leaves are smaller and stalkless

Fruit: thin green pod, turns brown, ½-¾" (1-2 cm) long

Bloom: summer

Cycle/Origin: perennial, native

Zone/Habitat: montane, subalpine, alpine; wet meadows, along streams and ponds

Range: western half of Colorado

Notes: Monkshood grows tall during a wet year. Flowers near the top of thin, flexible unbranched stems are smaller than those lower on the stalk. Sometimes was used in medicines, but the practice was discontinued when fatalities resulted. All plant parts (especially the roots) are extremely toxic and were used to poison bait in wolf traps during the settlement of the West, thus acquiring another common name, Wolfbane.

CLUSTER TYPE	FLOWER TYPE	LEAF TYPE	LEAF ATTACHMENT	FRUIT
Spike	Irregular	Simple Lobed	Alternate	Pod

RYDBERG PENSTEMON
Penstemon rydbergii

Family: Snapdragon (Scrophulariaceae)

Height: 10-24" (25-60 cm)

Flower: spike cluster, 2-6" (5-15 cm) long, of pale purple-to-blue-violet flowers; individual flower, ¾" (2 cm) long, has 3-lobed lower and 2-lobed upper lip; 1 of 5 flower parts (stamens) has hairy tip

Leaf: lance-shaped, 1-3" (2.5-7.5 cm) long, basally and oppositely attached; lower leaves have stalks, upper (cauline) leaves clasp the stem

Bloom: summer

Cycle/Origin: perennial, native

Zone/Habitat: all life zones except alpine; hillsides, forest openings, meadows

Range: throughout

Notes: There are at least 30 species of Penstemon native to the Rocky Mountains, with Rydberg Penstemon being common in Colorado. Many of these species hybridize with each other and make identification difficult. This plant is usually seen growing in clumps, with several stems arising from a large group of basal leaves. Look for the small pale purple flowers clustered at the end of the flower stalk to help identify. The genus name comes from the Greek *pente* for "five" and *stemon* for "thread," referring to the five stamens of the flower.

CLUSTER TYPE	FLOWER TYPE	LEAF TYPE	LEAF ATTACHMENT	LEAF ATTACHMENT	LEAF ATTACHMENT
Spike	Irregular	Simple	Opposite	Clasping	Basal

TALL PENSTEMON
Penstemon unilateralis

Family: Snapdragon (Scrophulariaceae)

Height: 12-28" (30-71 cm)

Flower: spike cluster, 2-6" (5-15 cm) long, of pinkish purple flowers; individual flower, ½-1" (1-2.5 cm) long, has 3-lobed lower and 2-lobed upper lip; flowers clustered on only one side of the stem

Leaf: narrow, 2-4" (5-10 cm) long, pointed tip, oppositely attached, clasping the stem

Bloom: summer

Cycle/Origin: perennial, native

Zone/Habitat: foothills, montane; hillsides, along roads, sandy slopes

Range: western half of Colorado

Notes: Also known as Tall Beardtongue, this common plant grows in abundance along Colorado roads in the foothills. Distinguished from other penstemons since all the flowers are clustered on one side of the stout stem, hence it is also called One-sided Penstemon. Like all plants in the *Penstemon* genus, it has five flower parts (stamens), one of which is sterile and hairy. Its flowers are an important source of nectar for hummingbirds. Makes a great addition to rock gardens and can easily be grown from seed.

CLUSTER TYPE	FLOWER TYPE	LEAF TYPE	LEAF ATTACHMENT	LEAF ATTACHMENT
Spike	Irregular	Simple	Opposite	Clasping

DUSKY BEARDTONGUE
Penstemon whippleanus

Family: Snapdragon (Scrophulariaceae)

Height: 6-26" (15-66 cm)

Flower: spike cluster, 2-8" (5-20 cm) long, of deep purple-to-blackish flowers; each flower, ¾-1½" (2-4 cm) long, 3-lobed lower lip longer than 2-lobed upper lip, 5 flower parts (stamens), white lines inside, outside covered with fine hairs; clusters of nodding flowers spaced along upper half of hairless stem

Leaf: lance-shaped, 2-6" (5-15 cm) long, opposite attachment; lower leaves stalked, upper are stalkless

Bloom: summer, early fall

Cycle/Origin: perennial, native

Zone/Habitat: montane, subalpine, alpine; forest openings, meadows, roadsides, other open sites

Range: western half of Colorado

Notes: Many beardtongues look alike, but careful inspection of the flowers and stems will help to identify your species. Look for the clusters of dark purple (rarely white), five-lobed flowers nodding from thin hairless stems to identify Dusky Beardtongue. One of the five stamens is sterile and has a tuft of hair at the tip, hence "Beardtongue" in the common name. This wildflower can be easily grown in gardens from seeds. Also known as Whipple Penstemon, named after Amiel Whipple, a surveyor of the West in the 1800s.

CLUSTER TYPE	FLOWER TYPE	LEAF TYPE	LEAF ATTACHMENT
Spike	**Irregular**	**Simple**	**Opposite**

157

PURPLE FRINGE
Phacelia sericea

Family: Waterleaf (Hydrophyllaceae)

Height: 4-16" (10-40 cm)

Flower: spike cluster, 3-7" (7.5-18 cm) long, of purple flowers with numerous yellow-tipped protruding flower parts (stamens); individual flower, ¼" (.6 cm) wide, with hairy petal-like sepals; stamens look like pins in a pincushion

Leaf: lobed, 1-6" (2.5-15 cm) long, deeply cut into many lobes, hairy; leaves are basally and alternately attached

Bloom: summer

Cycle/Origin: perennial, native

Zone/Habitat: montane, subalpine, alpine; rocky slopes, along roads, gravelly hills

Range: western half of Colorado

Notes: The long, yellow-tipped stamens protruding from Purple Fringe flowers bring pins in a pincushion to mind. It has many common names such as Silky Phacelia or Sky Pilot (not the Sky Pilot on pg. 143), as well as several containing the word "pincushion." Prefers to grow in high altitudes and is often found in clumps along roads or hiking trails. Can cause skin irritation if humans touch the plant, but elk eat it without problems.

CLUSTER TYPE	FLOWER TYPE	LEAF TYPE	LEAF ATTACHMENT	LEAF ATTACHMENT

Spike	**Regular**	**Simple Lobed**	**Alternate**	**Basal**

159

SUBALPINE LARKSPUR
Delphinium barbeyi

Family: Buttercup (Ranunculaceae)

Height: 4-6' (120-180 cm)

Flower: spike cluster, 4-8" (10-20 cm) long, of purple flowers; each flower, 1-1½" (2.5-4 cm) long, made of 5 sepals and 4 or 5 small inconspicuous petals; upper sepal forms a white spur; flowers are along the upper portion of a tall stem

Leaf: lobed, 4-8" (10-20 cm) long, divided into 5 or 7 deep lobes with pointed tips, smooth to the touch, basal and alternate attachment

Fruit: brown seedpod, 2-4" (5-10 cm) long

Bloom: summer

Cycle/Origin: perennial, native

Zone/Habitat: subalpine, alpine; moist meadows, along streams, wet forest openings

Range: western half of Colorado

Notes: The beautiful, star-shaped purple flowers add color to high, wet meadows. Even though attractive, larkspurs are generally not well liked by ranchers since they are toxic to livestock. Most plant parts contain poisonous alkaloids that can be fatal if ingested and should not be consumed or even touched by humans. Grows in large colonies in moist or wet conditions. Each taproot produces several sticky hairy stems, which are hollow and leafy.

CLUSTER TYPE	FLOWER TYPE	LEAF TYPE	LEAF ATTACHMENT	LEAF ATTACHMENT	FRUIT
Spike	**Irregular**	**Simple Lobed**	**Alternate**	**Basal**	**Pod**

PACIFIC ANEMONE
Anemone multifida

Family: Buttercup (Ranunculaceae)

Height: 8-20" (20-50 cm)

Flower: pinkish red (rarely white), ½-¾" (1-2 cm) wide, made up of 5-8 petal-like sepals surrounding 35-100 yellow flower parts (stamens)

Leaf: lobed, 1-5" (2.5-13 cm) long, deeply lobed, basal attachment with long stalks; stalkless whorled leaves just under each flower, deeply divided with very narrow lobes, ⅛" (.3 cm) wide, covered with long silky hairs that make it look gray

Bloom: spring, summer

Cycle/Origin: perennial, native

Zone/Habitat: all life zones except plains; dry soils, meadows, forests, rocky or grassy slopes, along roads

Range: western half of Colorado

Notes: Plants in the genus *Anemone* produce protoanemonin, an oil that is severely irritating, and contact with the leaves should be avoided. Despite this, some American Indians used the boiled leaves to kill fleas and lice. A hairy grayish plant that usually grows in clumps, but can grow alone. "Anemone" is from the Greek *anemos*, meaning "wind," and refers to the flowers swaying in the breezes. *Anemos* is also another name for the Greek god Adonis, whose blood (according to mythology) gave rise to a European species of anemone. Also called Red Anemone or Cutleaf Anemone.

FLOWER TYPE	LEAF TYPE	LEAF ATTACHMENT	LEAF ATTACHMENT
Regular	Simple Lobed	Whorl	Basal

WESTERN RED COLUMBINE
Aquilegia elegantula

Family: Buttercup (Ranunculaceae)

Height: 10-14" (25-36 cm)

Flower: red-and-yellow, 1-2" (2.5-5 cm) long, made up of 5 red petals with thin red or yellow spurs and 5 rounded sepals that are red-and-yellow

Leaf: twice compound, divided into 3 leaflets on slender stalks; each leaflet, 1-2" (2.5-5 cm) wide, has 3 lobes

Fruit: pod-like, light brown container; ¾" (2 cm) long; container is hairy

Bloom: summer

Cycle/Origin: perennial, native

Zone/Habitat: montane, subalpine; moist sites, forests, on rocky hillsides

Range: western half of Colorado

Notes: A plant with gorgeous flowers, Western Red Columbine graces the mountains west of the Continental Divide. Species name *elegantula* is Latin for "elegant," and aptly describes the flowers. Sometimes hybridizes with Yellow Columbine (*A. flavescens*) (not shown), producing pink or yellowish flowers. The long spurs contain nectar, which can only be reached by long-tongued animals such as hummingbirds, butterflies and some moths. "Columbine" means "dove-like," referring to the petals, which slightly resemble a group of doves in flight.

FLOWER TYPE	LEAF TYPE	LEAF ATTACHMENT	FRUIT
Bell	Twice Compound	Basal	Pod

FAIRY TRUMPET
Ipomopsis aggregata

Family: Phlox (Polemoniaceae)

Height: 1-4' (30-120 cm)

Flower: red, 1-2" (2.5-5 cm) long, 5 pointed petals fuse to form a tube

Leaf: thin and narrow, 1-3" (2.5-7.5 cm) long, highly divided; leaves mainly basally attached the first year, basal with a few alternately attached leaves the second

Bloom: summer, early fall

Cycle/Origin: biennial, native

Zone/Habitat: foothills, montane; dry slopes, open forests, fields

Range: western half of Colorado

Notes: Fairy Trumpet is one of the most delicate and loveliest flowers in Colorado. The plant looks almost too fragile to survive in the dry habitat it prefers. Grows well from seed and is featured in rock gardens across the state. Also known as Skyrocket, Scarlet Gilia or Skunk Flower, the latter name referring to its odorous foliage. Attracts hummingbirds, whose heads become covered with pollen while hovering at the entrance to the flower. They then pollinate the next Fairy Trumpet flower they visit while feeding on nectar in the tube.

FLOWER TYPE	LEAF TYPE	LEAF ATTACHMENT	LEAF ATTACHMENT
Tube	**Simple**	**Alternate**	**Basal**

WINE CUP
Callirhoe involucrata

Family: Mallow (Malvaceae)

Height: 8-12" (20-30 cm)

Flower: deep red, 1-2½" (2.5-6 cm) wide, cup-shaped, made up of 5 shiny round overlapping petals with a white spot at the bases; petals surround a ball-like center of yellow flower parts (stamens)

Leaf: lobed, 1-3" (2.5-7.5 cm) wide; deeply lobed into 4-7 jagged-edged, irregular segments that are long and thin; alternately attached

Bloom: spring, summer

Cycle/Origin: perennial, native

Zone/Habitat: plains, foothills; in open woods, meadows and prairies, on slopes

Range: eastern half of Colorado

Notes: Also known as the Poppy Mallow, this is a plant of lower elevations and open spaces in Colorado. Its stems crawl along the ground to form a thick mat. Borne on long, thin hairy stalks, the delicate flowers open in the morning and close in the evening. Flowers are a nectar source for butterflies and bees. Once an insect pollinates the flower, it remains closed. A host plant for the Gray Hairstreak butterfly.

FLOWER TYPE	LEAF TYPE	LEAF ATTACHMENT

Regular	Simple Lobed	Alternate

INDIAN BLANKET
Gaillardia pulchella

Family: Aster (Asteraceae)

Height: 12-30" (30-76 cm)

Flower: red (rarely yellow) with 3-lobed yellow tips, 2-3½" (5-9 cm) wide, composed of 12-20 petals (ray flowers) and a domed dark reddish to maroon central disk (disk flowers); petal colors will vary

Leaf: lobed, 2-4" (5-10 cm) long, basally attached, clasping the stem; lance-shaped stem (cauline) leaves are alternately attached

Bloom: summer

Cycle/Origin: annual, native

Zone/Habitat: plains, foothills; dry meadows, sunny slopes, forest openings

Range: eastern half of Colorado

Notes: Indian Blanket in bloom is considered one of the prettiest plants in Colorado. Many people plant it in gardens for its showy red flowers, which attract butterflies and bees, and because it is heat and drought resistant. Indian Blanket is closely related to the mostly yellow Blanketflower (pg. 343); both share another common name, Firewheel. Unlike the perennial Blanketflower, Indian Blanket has an annual growth cycle. American Indians used the plant parts to treat digestive problems and congestion.

FLOWER TYPE	LEAF TYPE	LEAF ATTACHMENT	LEAF ATTACHMENT	LEAF ATTACHMENT
Composite	Simple Lobed	Alternate	Clasping	Basal

RED CLOVER
Trifolium pratense

Family: Pea or Bean (Fabaceae)

Height: 6-24" (15-60 cm)

Flower: round cluster, 1" (2.5 cm) wide, of 50-100 rosy red flowers; each flower, ⅛-¼" (.3-.6 cm) long; appears as 1 large red flower

Leaf: typical clover leaf, ½-2" (1-5 cm) wide, made up of 3 leaflets; each leaflet has white markings in a V shape (chevron)

Bloom: spring, summer, fall

Cycle/Origin: perennial, non-native

Zone/Habitat: plains, foothills, montane; wet or dry soils, pastures, old fields, sun

Range: throughout

Notes: A native of Europe, Red Clover was introduced to North America as a hay and pasture crop. It has since escaped to the wild and is now one of the most common roadside plants. It is still grown as a rotation crop to improve the soil fertility because its roots fix nitrogen into the soil. The genus name *Trifolium* means "three leaves," which describes the three leaflets, while the species name *pratense* means "meadows," and refers to where you find it growing. Pollinated nearly exclusively by Honeybees. Without these insects, it is unable to produce seeds and will eventually die out. Seeds can lay dormant for years before sprouting.

CLUSTER TYPE	FLOWER TYPE	LEAF TYPE	LEAF ATTACHMENT
Round	Irregular	Compound	Alternate

QUEEN'S CROWN
Rhodiola rhodantha

Family: Stonecrop (Crassulaceae)

Height: 6-12" (15-30 cm)

Flower: round cluster, ½-2½" (1-6 cm) wide, of red-to-dark pink flowers at the end of stem; each flower is tiny, made up of 5 pointed petals and 5 small petal-like sepals

Leaf: lance-shaped, 1-1½" (2.5-4 cm) long, fleshy and alternately attached

Bloom: summer

Cycle/Origin: perennial, native

Zone/Habitat: subalpine, alpine; wet areas, in bogs and seeps, along streams

Range: western half of Colorado

Notes: This species is closely related to the burnt red-flowered King's Crown (*R. rosea*) (not shown), which shares wet habitats with Queen's Crown. Look for the larger, fire engine red-to-dark pink flower clusters to help distinguish between these species. Given the right wet habitat, this wildflower will bloom profusely in large colonies in the Colorado high country. Flowers are pollinated by insects, but can also self-pollinate when necessary. The plant has much foliage; the young leaves can be eaten raw or cooked and are high in vitamins A and C.

CLUSTER TYPE	FLOWER TYPE	LEAF TYPE	LEAF ATTACHMENT

Round	Regular	Simple	Alternate

PINEDROPS
Pterospora andromedea

Family: Indian Pipe (Monotropaceae)

Height: 1-3' (30-90 cm)

Flower: loose spike cluster, 1-4" (2.5-10 cm) long, of red-stemmed bell flowers nodding along a red stalk; each flower, ¼" (.6 cm) long, ovate, dull white to light pink to off-yellow; plant is covered with tiny hairs and appears overall reddish

Leaf: scale-like, ½-1" (.6-2.5 cm) long, brown and hairy, alternately attached

Bloom: summer

Cycle/Origin: annual, native

Zone/Habitat: foothills, montane; conifer forests, especially those with lots of organic debris

Range: western half of Colorado

Notes: This odd plant is one of a very few species that lacks the pigment chlorophyll, which gives plants their green color. Because of this, Pinedrops appear entirely reddish, whitish or purplish. The plant obtains nutrients from dead or decaying material in the soil (saprophytic). Found only in rich soils and usually among coniferous trees, which drop lots of organic matter to the ground. Grows for just one season, but the dried stems will sometimes persist for several years. Its tiny winged seeds are spread by strong breezes.

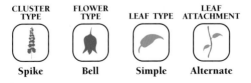

CLUSTER TYPE	FLOWER TYPE	LEAF TYPE	LEAF ATTACHMENT
Spike	Bell	Simple	Alternate

GIANT RED PAINTBRUSH
Castilleja miniata

Family: Snapdragon (Scrophulariaceae)

Height: 1-3' (30-90 cm)

Flower: spike cluster, 2-4" (5-10 cm) long, of inconspicuous green flowers interspersed among bright scarlet red bracts; bracts have 3 deep lobes

Leaf: lance-shaped, 1-3" (2.5-7.5 cm) long, alternately attached

Fruit: pod-like green container, turning brown with age, ¾" (2 cm) long, contains seeds

Bloom: summer

Cycle/Origin: perennial, native

Zone/Habitat: foothills, montane, subalpine; in aspen groves and meadows

Range: western half of Colorado

Notes: The most common paintbrush in Colorado. Spikes of bright red flowers sometimes appear to blanket the entire ground beneath aspen stands in a gorgeous show of nature's beauty. Also called Scarlet Paintbrush, referring to the color of the bracts. Like most paintbrushes, Giant Red is a partial parasite. Absorbs nutrients from the roots of other plants, especially aspen trees, to survive. Paintbrushes are an important source of high energy nectar for hummingbirds in the state.

CLUSTER TYPE	FLOWER TYPE	LEAF TYPE	LEAF ATTACHMENT	FRUIT
Spike	Tube	Simple	Alternate	Pod

ALPINE SANDWORT
Minuartia obtusiloba

Family: Pink (Caryophyllaceae)

Height: 1-2" (2.5-5 cm)

Flower: white, ⅜" (.9 cm) long, made up of 5 petals and 5 hairy brown petal-like sepals; each petal has an irregular tooth-like edge

Leaf: tiny, less than ¼" (.6 cm) long, basally attached; leaves are tightly clustered together and form a mat

Bloom: summer

Cycle/Origin: perennial, native

Zone/Habitat: alpine; dry, sandy or rocky soils, talus slopes

Range: western half of Colorado

Notes: Alpine Sandwort is a mat-forming plant of the high country. Looks similar to moss and can cover much surface area, but never gets very tall. Sometimes confused with the much taller Field Mouse Chickweed (pg. 197). This plant grows particularly well in sandy or rocky areas. An Arctic species, it ranges southward into the Rocky Mountains and extends as far south as New Mexico. The genus name *Minuartia* is in honor of Spanish botanist Juan Minuart. A tea can be made from its tiny leaves. Also called Twinflower Sandwort.

FLOWER TYPE	LEAF TYPE	LEAF ATTACHMENT	LEAF ATTACHMENT
Tube	Twice Compound	Opposite	Basal

ALPINE PHLOX
Phlox condensata

Family: Phlox (Polemoniaceae)

Height: 1-2" (2.5-5 cm)

Flower: bright white to very pale blue, ¼-½" (.6-1 cm) wide, made up of 5 petals that fuse together at the base to form a short tiny tube

Leaf: triangular, less than ½" (1 cm) long, fleshy, oppositely attached; leaves overlap, forming a mat

Bloom: summer

Cycle/Origin: perennial, native

Zone/Habitat: alpine; rocky tundra, open slopes, among rocks on mountain ridges

Range: western half of Colorado

Notes: Mats or cushions of Alpine Phlox grow low because of damaging alpine winds, but can cover lots of surface area. The flowers are extremely fragrant, attracting high altitude pollinators such as bees, moths and butterflies. *Phlox* is Greek for "flame," referring to fiery-colored flowers of some in the genus. There are about 300 species in the Phlox family, and many are cultivated for rock gardens across the West. Alpine Phlox, however, does well only in high altitude rock gardens. Also known as Dwarf Phlox.

FLOWER TYPE	LEAF TYPE	LEAF ATTACHMENT
Regular	Simple	Opposite

TASSELFLOWER
Brickellia grandiflora

Family: Aster (Asteraceae)

Height: 1-3' (30-90 cm)

Flower: off-white to light yellow; ⅜-½" (.9-1 cm) long, of disk flowers only with light green bracts; nodding flowers found in groups

Leaf: triangular, 1-5" (2.5-13 cm) long, coarsely toothed, underside is covered with fine hairs, alternately attached

Bloom: summer, fall

Cycle/Origin: perennial, native

Zone/Habitat: foothills, montane; canyons, forests, rocky slopes

Range: western half of Colorado

Notes: Tasselflower is very common in canyons of the Colorado foothills. Can grow somewhat bushy, hence it is also known as Brickellbush. Some consider the native Tasselflower a weed, but it will not spread uncontrollably. Genus name *Brickellia* honors Dr. John Brickell, an early American naturalist. Species name *grandiflora* means "large-flowered," which in this case may be a misnomer.

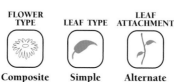

FLOWER TYPE — **Composite** LEAF TYPE — **Simple** LEAF ATTACHMENT — **Alternate**

WHITE PRAIRIE ASTER
Symphyotrichum falcatum

Family: Aster (Asteraceae)

Height: 2-3' (60-90 cm)

Flower: white, ½" (1 cm) wide, composed of 15-25 petals (ray flowers) surrounding a yellow center (disk flowers)

Leaf: long and thin, 1-3" (2.5-7.5 cm) long, oppositely attached; numerous leaves on wiry stems

Bloom: late summer, fall

Cycle/Origin: perennial, native

Zone/Habitat: plains, foothills; wooded openings, fields, along roads

Range: eastern half of Colorado

Notes: White Prairie Aster has endured changes to both its genus and species names, and it is known by many different common names. In Colorado, also called Rough White Aster or Tufted White Aster. A late-blooming plant that forms a tangled mass of stems and flower heads. Spreads by horizontal underground stems (rhizomes). American Indians used the stems and leaves to make lotions to help cure snakebite. Looks similar to Many-flowered Aster (*S. ericoides*) (not shown).

FLOWER TYPE

Composite

LEAF TYPE

Simple

LEAF ATTACHMENT

Opposite

TRAILING FLEABANE
Erigeron flagellaris

Family: Aster (Asteraceae)

Height: 8-12" (20-30 cm)

Flower: white, ½-¾" (1-2 cm) wide, composed of numerous thin petals (ray flowers) surrounding a yellow center (disk flowers)

Leaf: spoon-shaped, 1-2" (2.5-5 cm) long, smooth and soft, basally attached; upper (cauline) are alternately attached; leaves are mainly basal with fewer smaller upper leaves

Bloom: spring, summer

Cycle/Origin: biennial, native

Zone/Habitat: all life zones except alpine; open areas, hillsides, prairies

Range: throughout

Notes: Trailing Fleabane is very common in open sites throughout Colorado. Known by many common names such as Trailing Daisy or Whiplash Daisy, the latter referring to the motion of the tall twisting stems in gusts of summer winds. Species name *flagellaris* means "whip" and refers to the runners the plant produces each growing season, some of which take root. "Fleabane" comes from an ancient myth that these plants repelled fleas. An important nectar source for small butterflies and other insects.

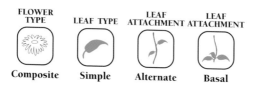

FLOWER TYPE	LEAF TYPE	LEAF ATTACHMENT	LEAF ATTACHMENT
Composite	Simple	Alternate	Basal

fruit

WILD STRAWBERRY
Fragaria virginiana

Family: Rose (Roseaceae)

Height: 3-6" (7.5-15 cm)

Flower: white, ¾" (2 cm) wide, 5 round petals surrounding a yellow center; in groups of 2-10 flowers

Leaf: 3-parted, 3" (7.5 cm) wide, basally attached; each leaflet, 1" (2.5 cm) long, coarsely toothed; leaf sits on a hairy stalk

Fruit: green berry, turning bright red, ¼-½" (.6-1 cm) wide

Bloom: spring, summer

Cycle/Origin: perennial, native

Zone/Habitat: foothills, montane, subalpine; dry soils, edges of woods, sun

Range: western half of Colorado

Notes: The original species from which cultivated strawberries are derived and one of several species of strawberry in Colorado. Primary means of reproduction is through underground runners; by seed is a secondary method. Often growing in large patches, Wild Strawberry produces some of the sweetest tasting wild berries. The berry is actually the enlarged central portion of the flower and is covered with embedded seeds. Its flowers and fruit are always on stems separate from the leaves. The leaves have a high amount of vitamin C and can be used for making tea.

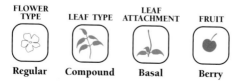

FLOWER TYPE	LEAF TYPE	LEAF ATTACHMENT	FRUIT
Regular	Compound	Basal	Berry

COMMON ALP LILY
Lloydia serotina

Family: Lily (Liliaceae)

Height: 2-6" (5-15 cm)

Flower: mostly white, ¾" (2 cm) wide, made up of 3 petals, 3 petal-like sepals (often mistaken for petals) and a yellowish center; petals have purple or green veins

Leaf: slender and grass-like, up to 6" (15 cm) long, basal attachment; leaves can grow as long as flower stem

Bloom: summer

Cycle/Origin: perennial, native

Zone/Habitat: alpine; near rocks, crevices, among gravelly ridges

Range: western half of Colorado

Notes: Common Alp Lily, also known as Alpine Lily, is an arctic species that manages to survive in the Colorado tundra. A common plant that can be found growing singly or in small groups. Its blooms have purple or green veins that reflect ultraviolet light and attract flies and other insects, which pollinate the flowers. Has a bulb-like taproot in which it stores much of its energy. The only native species in the genus *Lloydia*. Please do not pick the flowers or dig up or trample this fragile plant.

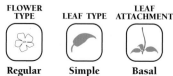

FLOWER TYPE	LEAF TYPE	LEAF ATTACHMENT
Regular	Simple	Basal

ROCKY MOUNTAIN PHLOX
Phlox multiflora

Family: Phlox (Polemoniaceae)

Height: 4-8" (10-20 cm)

Flower: white (rarely pink), ¾" (2 cm) wide, made up of 5 broad, slightly pointed or rounded petals that form a slender tube

Leaf: thin, ¼-½" (.6-1 cm) long, oppositely attached; overlapping leaves form mats that appear like moss

Bloom: spring, early summer

Cycle/Origin: perennial, native

Zone/Habitat: plains, foothills, montane; dry areas, along roads, rocky hillsides

Range: western half of Colorado

Notes: Rocky Mountain Phlox never grows very tall, but can still "stop traffic" when blooming near the road. The leaves form large cushions or mats, but the white (rarely pink) flowers can be so numerous, they completely hide the tiny leaves. Flowers are pollinated by insects, especially hummingbird moths. Grazing mammals such as deer and elk eat this plant. Some American Indians used a mixture of the crushed leaves and flowers as a stimulant. *Phlox* is the Greek word for "flame," and refers to the brightly colored flowers in the genus. This plant is also known as Flowery Phlox.

FLOWER TYPE	LEAF TYPE	LEAF ATTACHMENT
Regular	Simple	Opposite

FIELD MOUSE CHICKWEED
Cerastium arvense

Family: Pink (Caryophyllaceae)

Height: 3-12" (7.5-30 cm)

Flower: white, ½-1" (1-2.5 cm) long, made up of 5 deeply notched petals and yellow flower parts (stamens); flowers in loose groupings

Leaf: lance-shaped, 1" (2.5 cm) long, covered with velvety hairs, oppositely attached

Fruit: tapered cylindrical green capsule, turning brown, ½" (1 cm) long

Bloom: spring, summer

Cycle/Origin: perennial, native

Zone/Habitat: all life zones; grassy areas, dry hills, meadows and forest openings

Range: throughout

Notes: A common plant that blooms very early in the Colorado plains and foothills. Sometimes Field Mouse Chickweed will grow in large patches, attracting butterflies and other pollinating insects. Called "Chickweed" because these plants were often fed to domestic chickens and other barnyard birds. The genus name *Cerastium*, from the Greek *kerastes*, refers to the shape of the seed capsule, which is sometimes bent or "horned."

FLOWER TYPE	LEAF TYPE	LEAF ATTACHMENT	FRUIT
Tube	Simple	Opposite	Pod

NIGHT-FLOWERING CATCHFLY
Silene noctiflora

Family: Pink (Caryophyllaceae)

Height: 2-3' (60-90 cm)

Flower: white, ½-1" (1-2.5 cm) wide, with 5 notched petals; oblong green- and red-veined "bladder" (calyx) behind flower

Leaf: lance-shaped, 1-3" (2.5-7.5 cm) long, hairy and oppositely attached

Fruit: cylindrical green seed capsule, turning brown, ¼-½" (.6-1 cm) long

Bloom: spring, summer, fall

Cycle/Origin: annual, non-native

Zone/Habitat: plains, foothills, montane; disturbed soils, along roads, in vacant fields

Range: throughout

Notes: Night-flowering Catchfly was introduced to North America from Europe and has now spread throughout the West. The species name *noctiflora* is Latin and means "flowering at night." Attracts night-flying moths, which feed on the nectar and pollinate the flowers. Flower resembles a tiny decorative lantern or half-inflated balloon. The genus *Silene* was named by Swedish botanist Carolus Linnaeus. Also known as Night-flowering Silene.

FLOWER TYPE	LEAF TYPE	LEAF ATTACHMENT	FRUIT
Regular	Simple	Opposite	Pod

WOOD NYMPH
Moneses uniflora

Family: Wintergreen (Pyrolaceae)

Height: 3-5" (7.5-13 cm)

Flower: dull white, ½-1" (1-2.5 cm) wide, star-shaped, composed of 5 petals and a large green flower part (pistil); 1 flower per plant; flower nods from stem, looks waxy and is very fragrant

Leaf: round, ½-1" (1-2.5 cm) wide, on stalk, whorled, basally attached; leaves are evergreen

Bloom: summer

Cycle/Origin: perennial, native

Zone/Habitat: montane, subalpine; moist forests, shady places along streams

Range: western half of Colorado

Notes: Wood Nymph is a plant of shady moist forests and may go unnoticed by all but the most observant hikers. Once found, this fragrant beauty should be enjoyed, but do not pick the single flower. This plant needs dark or wet conditions in which to grow and prefers habitats such as moss mounds or near springs or seeps. Known by many common names, including Shy Maiden or Waxflower. Another common name, Single Delight, and the genus name *Moneses* come from two Greek words that when combined mean "single delight," referring to the plant's one flower.

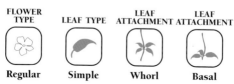

FLOWER TYPE	LEAF TYPE	LEAF ATTACHMENT	LEAF ATTACHMENT
Regular	Simple	Whorl	Basal

MOUNTAIN DRYAD
Dryas octopetala

Family: Rose (Rosaceae)

Height: 4-8" (10-20 cm); low shrub

Flower: off-white, 1" (2.5 cm) wide, with 8 (usually) petals surrounding a group of yellow parts (stamens)

Leaf: wedge-shaped or oval, 1-1½" (2.5-4 cm) long, leathery, lobed margins, dense hairs on underside, basally and alternately attached

Bloom: summer

Cycle/Origin: perennial, native

Zone/Habitat: alpine; exposed ridges, rocky slopes, tundra

Range: western half of Colorado

Notes: Mountain Dryad is a low evergreen shrub of the alpine zone. It can form dense mats that cover much surface area, but never grows very tall. "Ground-hugging" is a characteristic that helps protect Mountain Dryad from the strong, bitter cold tundra winds. The thick leaves with their often curled edges can help identify the plant when not in bloom. The species name *octopetala* means "eight petals," the usual number for this plant. "Dryad" in the common name refers to a wood nymph or mythical fairy who lives in forests.

FLOWER TYPE

Regular

LEAF TYPE

Simple

LEAF ATTACHMENT

Alternate

LEAF ATTACHMENT

Basal

SPREADING FLEABANE
Erigeron divergens

Family: Aster (Asteraceae)

Height: 6-24" (15-60 cm)

Flower: white to light pink, 1" (2.5 cm) wide, composed of numerous (up to 100) petals (ray flowers) that surround a yellow center (disk flowers); flowers sit atop many branched hairy stems

Leaf: lance-shaped, ½-2" (1-5 cm) long, hairy, alternately attached

Bloom: spring, summer, fall

Cycle/Origin: biennial, native

Zone/Habitat: plains, foothills, montane; open sites, sandy woods, valleys, along roads

Range: throughout

Notes: Spreading Fleabane is a common plant in Colorado usually seen growing in disturbed sites such as roadsides and the edges of parking lots. Extremely drought tolerant, and once established in an area, it needs very little water. Can be confused with Trailing Fleabane (pg. 189), but has densely hairy leaves and stems, while those of Trailing Fleabane are smooth. Unlike Trailing Fleabane, which usually grows singly, Spreading Fleabane mostly grows in large clumps. The species name *divergens* means "spreading out widely from the center," which accurately describes its growth.

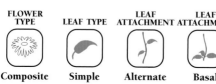

FLOWER TYPE	LEAF TYPE	LEAF ATTACHMENT	LEAF ATTACHMENT
Composite	Simple	Alternate	Basal

BLACKHEAD FLEABANE
Erigeron melanocephalus

Family: Aster (Asteraceae)

Height: 3-6" (7.5-15 cm)

Flower: white, 1-1½" (2.5-4 cm) wide, made up of numerous petals (ray flowers) surrounding a large domed yellow center (disk flowers); bracts are covered with black hairs and appear woolly

Leaf: spoon-shaped, 1½" (4 cm) long, stalked; leaves are mainly basally attached, upper (cauline) leaves are smaller and alternately attached

Bloom: summer

Cycle/Origin: perennial, native

Zone/Habitat: subalpine, alpine; moist meadows, tundra slopes, near melting snow

Range: western half of Colorado

Notes: A plant of high elevations, Blackhead Fleabane sprouts and blooms soon after the mountain snows starts to melt, completing its growing cycle quickly out of necessity. Like most alpine plants, it stores much energy in its large taproot. "Blackhead" in the common name and the species name *melanocephalus* refer to the woolly black hairs that cover the bracts. Some American Indians crushed and cooked the plant, then added it to grease to make a salve for treating wounds. Also called Black-headed Daisy.

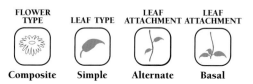

FLOWER TYPE	LEAF TYPE	LEAF ATTACHMENT	LEAF ATTACHMENT
Composite	Simple	Alternate	Basal

LARGE MOUNTAIN FLEABANE
Erigeron coulteri

Family: Aster (Asteraceae)

Height: 1-2' (30-60 cm)

Flower: white, 1-1½" (2.5-4 cm) wide, made up of numerous petals (ray flowers) surrounding a large domed yellow center (disk flowers); bracts are covered with long dark hairs

Leaf: lance-shaped, 4-7" (10-18 cm) long, hairy, finely toothed, alternately attached; stalked lower leaves

Bloom: summer

Cycle/Origin: perennial, native

Zone/Habitat: foothills, montane, subalpine; moist meadows, stream banks

Range: western half of Colorado

Notes: Because its flowers look similar to daisies, refer to the leaves and stems of Large Mountain Fleabane to help identify. Look for the large, lance-shaped leaves with fine teeth and the leafy hairy stems. The genus *Erigeron* was named in the 1700s by the father of botany, Carolus Linnaeus. Species name *coulteri* was named for botanist John Coulter, who, along with Thomas Porter, penned the first field guide for the flora of Colorado.

FLOWER TYPE

Composite

LEAF TYPE

Simple

LEAF ATTACHMENT

Alternate

CREAMY THISTLE
Cirsium canescens

Family: Aster (Asteraceae)

Height: 12-32" (30-80 cm)

Flower: creamy white, 1-1½" (2.5-4 cm) wide, composed of only disk flowers encased by spine-tipped, dark green bracts

Leaf: lobed, 4-8" (10-20 cm) long, lobes are deeply cut, twisted, spines of various sizes all along margin, alternately attached

Bloom: summer, early fall

Cycle/Origin: perennial, native

Zone/Habitat: plains, foothills, montane; forest openings, along roads, on canyon slopes

Range: throughout

Notes: Creamy Thistle is a common plant in the Colorado foothills, although it also occurs in the plains and montane life zones. As with all thistles, it is not a pleasant plant to touch or brush up against. Look for the stout branching stem with cobweb-like hairs that distinguishes it from other thistles. Genus name *Cirsium* comes from a Greek word meaning "swollen vein," a condition for which thistles were thought to be a cure. Bees are its chief pollinators, although hummingbirds will also pollinate the flowers while seeking nectar. Also known as Prairie Thistle.

FLOWER TYPE
Composite

LEAF TYPE
Simple Lobed

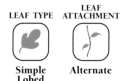
LEAF ATTACHMENT
Alternate

SAND LILY
Leucocrinum montanum

Family: Lily (Liliaceae)

Height: 4-8" (10-20 cm)

Flower: bright white, 1-1½" (2.5-4 cm) wide, made of 6 lance-shaped, petal-like segments fused together to form a long tube that surrounds 6 pollen-covered flower parts (stamens)

Leaf: folded, narrow and grass-like, 2-8" (5-20 cm) long, basally attached

Bloom: spring, summer

Cycle/Origin: perennial, native

Zone/Habitat: plains, foothills; open forests, fields, among sagebrush on the prairie

Range: throughout

Notes: Sand Lily grows in bunches, emerging from conspicuous clumps of grass-like leaves. The star-shaped white flowers are among the first to push up through the soil each spring. Flowers look and feel waxy, and their long tubes actually attach to the stems underground. The seed capsule from the previous year starts just below the ground and is pushed up by the subsequent year's flower buds, spreading the seeds. The genus name *Leucocrinum* is derived from the Greek words for "white" and "lily." Also known as Star Lily, named for the shape of the flowers.

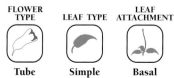

FLOWER TYPE	LEAF TYPE	LEAF ATTACHMENT
Tube	Simple	Basal

ELKWEED
Frasera speciosa

Family: Gentian (Gentianaceae)

Height: 3-6' (90-180 cm)

Flower: off-white to light green, 1-1½" (2.5-4 cm) wide, 4 oval petals join at the base; flowers grouped along stem and among the leaves

Leaf: lance-shaped, 2-16" (5-40 cm) long; basally attached the first year, whorled attachment the second; larger leaves toward lower portions of stems

Bloom: summer

Cycle/Origin: biennial, native

Zone/Habitat: foothills, montane, subalpine; open or shaded areas, in fields, along roads

Range: western half of Colorado

Notes: A tall plant and cone-shaped, like a thin Christmas tree. The flowers, which attract insect pollinators, are densely packed along the upper part of this single-stemmed plant. Called Elkweed because it is a favorite plant for elk to browse upon, but deer also eat the leaves. Also known as Green Gentian, Monument Plant or Deer's Ears, the latter name referring to the shape of the leaves. Navajo Indians sometimes used the leaves in smoking ceremonies.

FLOWER TYPE	LEAF TYPE	LEAF ATTACHMENT	LEAF ATTACHMENT
Regular	Simple	Whorl	Basal

GLOBEFLOWER
Trollius laxus

Family: Buttercup (Ranunculaceae)

Height: 6-20" (15-50 cm)

Flower: creamy white, 1-1½" (2.5-4 cm) wide, saucer-shaped, made up of 5-8 rounded, petal-like sepals surrounding a group of yellow plant parts (stamens and pistils)

Leaf: lobed, 1½-3½" (4-9 cm) wide, deeply divided into 5-7 sharply toothed lobes, basally and alternately attached; basal leaves are stalked, stem leaves can be stalked or stalkless

Bloom: spring, summer

Cycle/Origin: perennial, native

Zone/Habitat: montane, subalpine, alpine; wet meadows, moist forest openings, along streams, near melting snow

Range: western half of Colorado

Notes: All parts of Globeflower are poisonous and should never be eaten. During a wet growing season, Globeflower plants can be found in large clumps in the mountains, even ranging into the alpine zone. Each hairless stem will have only one flower. Genus name *Trollius* is from the German *trol*, meaning "round," and refers to the rounded shape of the sepals. Attracts butterflies and other insect pollinators. The flowers look similar to the White Marsh Marigold (pg. 219), but Globeflower leaves are deeply lobed, while those of the White Marsh Marigold are heart-shaped.

FLOWER TYPE	LEAF TYPE	LEAF ATTACHMENT	LEAF ATTACHMENT

Regular	**Simple Lobed**	**Alternate**	**Basal**

WHITE MARSH MARIGOLD
Caltha leptosepala

Family: Buttercup (Ranunculaceae)

Height: 2-10" (5-25 cm)

Flower: white, 1½" (4 cm) wide, made up of 5-15 greenish-veined, petal-like sepals that surround a central group of yellow flower parts; flower lacks petals

Leaf: round or oval, 2-3" (5-7.5 cm) wide, finely toothed, deeply notched where long stalk attaches, basally attached

Bloom: summer

Cycle/Origin: perennial, native

Zone/Habitat: subalpine, alpine; in marshy areas, bogs and wet meadows, near melting snow banks

Range: western half of Colorado

Notes: The White Marsh Marigold is common in the Colorado mountains, especially along melting snow banks and in wet meadows. Also called Elk's Lip because of the shape of the leaves. Some herbalists say the leaves are edible after cooking and liken them to sauerkraut; others warn against eating any part of the plant. Elk, deer and moose eat the leaves and blooms when available.

FLOWER TYPE	LEAF TYPE	LEAF ATTACHMENT
Regular	**Simple**	**Basal**

MARIPOSA LILY
Calochortus gunnisonii

Family: Lily (Liliaceae)

Height: 10-18" (25-45 cm)

Flower: white (rarely light pink), 1-2" (2.5-5 cm) wide, cup-shaped, made up of 3 broad petals and 3 narrow petal-like sepals with pointed tips; petals have a purple band and yellow hairs near bases inside the flower cup

Leaf: grass-like, 3-12" (7.5-30 cm) long, basally and alternately attached

Bloom: spring, summer

Cycle/Origin: perennial, native

Zone/Habitat: foothills, montane, subalpine; aspen groves, forest openings, meadows

Range: western half of Colorado

Notes: Mariposa Lily grows in patches and has tall thin flower stalks that sway in the slightest breeze. The stems branch several times and have several delicate flowers with petals that also flutter in the wind. Taproot is edible and was eaten by Ute Indians, who in turn taught Mormon settlers to use it for food. Genus name *Calochortus* is derived from the Greek words for "beautiful" and "grass," referring to the thin leaves. Also known as Sego Lily.

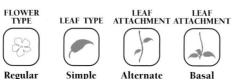

FLOWER TYPE	LEAF TYPE	LEAF ATTACHMENT	LEAF ATTACHMENT
Regular	Simple	Alternate	Basal

fruit

THIMBLEBERRY
Rubus parviflorus

Family: Rose (Roseaceae)

Height: 3-6' (90-180 cm); shrub

Flower: white, 1-2" (2.5-5 cm) wide, with 5 petals and numerous yellow flower parts in the center; one flower per stem, can have numerous flowers blooming at same time

Leaf: maple-shaped, 4-8" (10-20 cm) long, 5 lobes with numerous sharp teeth and deep veins, alternately attached along the stems

Fruit: green berry, turning red when ripe, $\frac{3}{4}$-$1\frac{1}{4}$" (2-3 cm) wide; looks similar to a very large raspberry

Bloom: spring, summer

Cycle/Origin: perennial, native

Zone/Habitat: foothills, montane, subalpine; woodland edges, cool damp ravines and canyons

Range: western half of Colorado

Notes: A woody shrub that often grows along edges of woodlands where there is enough sunlight to survive. The large showy flowers produce raspberry-like fruit big enough to fit over a finger like a sewing thimble, hence the common name. The fruit is edible and excellent for making jam or eating directly off the plant.

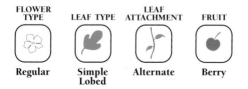

FLOWER TYPE	LEAF TYPE	LEAF ATTACHMENT	FRUIT
Regular	Simple Lobed	Alternate	Berry

FIELD BINDWEED
Convolvulus arvensis

Family: Morning Glory (Convolvulaceae)

Height: 1-6' (30-180 cm); climbing vine

Flower: white, 1-2" (2.5-5 cm) wide, 5 petals fuse together to form the tube or funnel-shaped flower

Leaf: triangular or arrowhead-shaped, 1-2" (2.5-5 cm) long, small and toothless, alternately attached along the climbing, twisting stem

Bloom: spring, summer, fall

Cycle/Origin: perennial, non-native

Zone/Habitat: plains, foothills; dry soils, sunny fields, usually creeps along the ground, but occasionally climbs on fences or shrubs

Range: eastern half of Colorado

Notes: This wildflower is usually so small that it goes unnoticed until its pure white flowers open on sunny days. Closely related to the Common Blue Morning Glory of the garden, Field Bindweed prefers disturbed soils, old fields, abandoned lots in cities and suburban lawns. It grows in large tangled mats, with the flowers sometimes slightly pink. The genus name *Convolvulus* comes from the Latin word *convolvere*, meaning "to entwine," which accurately describes its growing habit. Lacking tendrils to grasp other plants, it seeks sunlight by twisting its stems around host plants for support, a habit that provides its other common name, Possession Vine.

FLOWER
TYPE

Tube

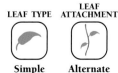

LEAF TYPE

Simple

LEAF
ATTACHMENT

Alternate

ARCTIC GENTIAN
Gentiana algida

Family: Gentian (Gentianaceae)

Height: 2-8" (5-20 cm)

Flower: off-white to light green, 1-2" (2.5-5 cm) long, funnel-shaped; petals have purple streaks and dots

Leaf: narrowly lance-shaped, 2-4" (5-10 cm) long, lacks a stalk, oppositely attached

Bloom: late summer

Cycle/Origin: perennial, native

Zone/Habitat: subalpine, alpine; wet and moist meadows, along streams, near ponds

Range: western half of Colorado

Notes: Arctic Gentian is one of the last wildflowers to bloom in the alpine zone and gives the tundra a bit of color well into August, when most other flowers have already gone to seed. Thus, it provides a late-summer nectar source for butterflies and other insects. For perhaps thousands of years, gentians have been used for medicinal remedies, including as an ingredient in a tonic for appetite stimulation. However, ingesting large amounts of the mixture can cause nausea or vomiting. Also called Whitish Gentian.

FLOWER TYPE	LEAF TYPE	LEAF ATTACHMENT
Tube	**Simple**	**Opposite**

EASTER DAISY
Townsendia hookeri

Family: Aster (Asteraceae)

Height: 2-4" (5-10 cm)

Flower: white, 1-2" (2.5-5 cm) wide, composed of up to 40 petals (ray flowers) surrounding a yellow or tan center (disk flowers)

Leaf: thin, 1-3" (2.5-7.5 cm) long, gray, hairy, basally attached

Bloom: spring

Cycle/Origin: perennial, native

Zone/Habitat: plains, foothills; dry hillsides, sunny slopes, forest openings

Range: eastern half of Colorado

Notes: Easter Daisy is so named because of its blooming habit, which sometimes coincides with the Easter holiday in spring. Look for this beautiful flower on sandy hillsides and sunny slopes beginning as early as March. The flowers in full bloom with their yellow centers look spectacular (especially after a long Colorado winter without color), despite it being a low growing plant with basal leaves only. Navajo Indians used the Easter Daisy extensively in ritualistic ceremonies, particularly those relating to childbirth. Also called Hooker Townsend Daisy after the early 1800s botanist William Hooker.

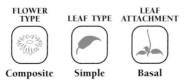

FLOWER TYPE	LEAF TYPE	LEAF ATTACHMENT
Composite	Simple	Basal

OXEYE DAISY
Leucanthemum vulgare

Family: Aster (Asteraceae)

Height: 1-3' (30-90 cm)

Flower: white-and-yellow, 1-2" (2.5-5 cm) wide, composed of up to 20 white petals (ray flowers) surrounding a yellow center of disk flowers

Leaf: lobed and dandelion-like, up to 6" (15 cm) long, thick, dark green, basally attached and clasping the stem; stem leaf, 1-2" (2.5-5 cm) long; stem leaves are similar to basal, but smaller

Bloom: spring, summer, fall

Cycle/Origin: perennial, non-native

Zone/Habitat: plains, foothills, montane; wet or dry soils, fields, along roads, pastures, sun

Range: throughout

Notes: Also called Common Daisy, the Oxeye Daisy is a European import often seen growing in patches along roads. In poor soil it grows short and erect; in rich soils it grows tall, and its weak stem causes it to fall over and spread out across the ground. Oxeye Daisy contains pyrethrum, a chemical that repels insects and is used in organic pesticides. This nice garden plant is often overlooked. An interesting composite of many flowers appearing as one large flower. Each white petal is considered a separate flower, while the center yellow portion is composed of many individual disk flowers.

FLOWER TYPE	LEAF TYPE	LEAF ATTACHMENT	LEAF ATTACHMENT	LEAF ATTACHMENT
Composite	Simple Lobed	Alternate	Clasping	Basal

SCENTLESS CHAMOMILE
Matricaria perforata

Family: Aster (Asteraceae)

Height: 12-30" (30-76 cm)

Flower: white, 2" (5 cm) wide, made up of 15-20 petals (ray flowers) surrounding a yellow center (disk flowers)

Leaf: lobed, 2-2.5" (5-6 cm) long, finely divided and feathery, alternately attached

Bloom: summer, fall

Cycle/Origin: annual, non-native

Zone/Habitat: montane, subalpine; disturbed ground, along roads, abandoned fields

Range: western half of Colorado

Notes: Scentless Chamomile is a daisy look-alike and appears very similar to Oxeye Daisy (pg. 231), but it has lobed leaves as opposed to the coarse-toothed leaves of Oxeye Daisy. Both wildflowers were introduced from Europe and can be seen growing in large numbers along Colorado roads. Although "Scentless" in the common name, it does have a faint pineapple scent that attracts flies. A tea can be made from the dried flowers. Efforts are being made to stop the spread of Scentless Chamomile, which has been listed as a noxious weed in Colorado.

FLOWER TYPE	LEAF TYPE	LEAF ATTACHMENT
Composite	Simple Lobed	Alternate

BOULDER RASPBERRY
Rubus deliciosus

Family: Rose (Roseaceae)

Height: 2-5' (60-150 cm); shrub

Flower: pale to bright white, 1-3" (2.5-7.5 cm) wide, with 5 delicate petals surrounding a center of yellow flower parts (stamens)

Leaf: lobed, 1-2½" (2.5-6 cm) long, has 3-5 lobes, toothed margin, alternately attached

Fruit: dry round green berry, turning purple, ½" (1 cm) wide; contains many seeds and lacks flavor

Bloom: summer

Cycle/Origin: perennial, native

Zone/Habitat: plains, foothills, montane; dry hillsides, along roads, on slopes

Range: throughout

Notes: Boulder Raspberry shrubs (also called brambles) are fairly common and can grow quite large. The shrub has an overall "messy" appearance–the branches are tangled and the bark of older stems splits and peels. Unlike other raspberry species, Boulder Raspberry branches lack spines. Species name *deliciosus* is somewhat of a misnomer, as the fruit is seedy, dry and certainly not tasty. Also known as Rocky Mountain Raspberry.

FLOWER TYPE	LEAF TYPE	LEAF ATTACHMENT	FRUIT
Regular	Simple Lobed	Alternate	Berry

PRICKLY POPPY
Argemone polyanthemos

Family: Poppy (Papaveraceae)

Height: 15-45" (38-114 cm)

Flower: white, 2-3" (5-7.5 cm) wide, composed of 4-6 thin round crumpled petals surrounding a ball-like center of yellow flower parts (stamens)

Leaf: lobed, 4-8" (10-20 cm) long, deep lobes, yellow spines along veins and edges, alternately attached

Fruit: spiny oval pod, remains green for 2-3 months, $\frac{3}{4}$-1" (2-2.5 cm) long

Bloom: spring, summer

Cycle/Origin: annual or perennial, native

Zone/Habitat: plains, foothills; dry slopes, along roads, hillsides

Range: eastern half of Colorado

Notes: When not in bloom, Prickly Poppy may be confused with a thistle plant because of its similar-looking leaves. However, its blooming white flowers are unmistakable. The delicate flowers attract many types of insect pollinators. Sometimes grows in huge groups, especially along eastern Colorado roads. All parts of Prickly Poppy are poisonous to humans and animals, but the plant is so prickly and distasteful that animals avoid it. Do not touch this plant–the yellow spines on the leaves are extremely sharp.

FLOWER TYPE

Regular

LEAF TYPE

Simple Lobed

LEAF ATTACHMENT

Alternate

FRUIT

Pod

TUFTED EVENING-PRIMROSE
Oenothera caespitosa

Family: Evening-primrose (Onagraceae)

Height: 2-6" (5-15 cm)

Flower: white, 3-4" (7.5-10 cm) wide, made up of 4 heart-shaped petals fused together into a long tube at the base and surrounding a group of yellow flower parts

Leaf: lance-shaped, 2-6" (5-15 cm) long, smooth or toothed edges, basally attached

Fruit: woody pod-like brown container, ½-2" (1-5 cm) long

Bloom: spring, summer

Cycle/Origin: perennial, native

Zone/Habitat: plains, foothills, montane; dry slopes along roads, sunny areas

Range: throughout

Notes: Tufted Evening-primrose can be seen along most roadways in Colorado, but it most commonly grows on dry, south-facing hillsides. "Evening" in the common name refers to its blooming habit. The flowers bloom during the evenings and wilt by noon the following day. Night-flying insects (usually moths) pollinate the flowers. The blooms are large and spectacular, especially when compared to the overall small size of the plant. Spreads by horizontal underground stems (rhizomes), which gives rise to new plants. The seeds are an important food for songbirds.

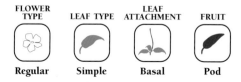

FLOWER TYPE	LEAF TYPE	LEAF ATTACHMENT	FRUIT
Regular	Simple	Basal	Pod

WHITE WATER-LILY
Nymphaea odorata

Family: Water-lily (Nymphaeaceae)

Height: aquatic

Flower: white, 3-6" (7.5-15 cm) wide, made of numerous pointed petals surrounding a yellow center; floats on the water

Leaf: round or heart-shaped, 5-12" (13-30 cm) wide, shiny green, deeply notched and toothless; floats on the water

Bloom: summer

Cycle/Origin: perennial, non-native

Zone/Habitat: plains, foothills; small lakes, channels, bays

Range: eastern half of Colorado

Notes: White Water-lily has been introduced into many slow-moving or calm bodies of water in eastern Colorado. The leaves float directly on the surface of still water and sometimes are referred to as lily pads. This common water-lily requires quiet water, rooting to bottoms of ponds and lakes. Roots produce large horizontal stems (rhizomes), which are often eaten by muskrats. Its vertical stems and its leaves have air channels that trap air to keep the plant afloat. Flowers open on sunny days, closing at night and on cloudy days. Also called Fragrant Water-lily.

FLOWER
TYPE

LEAF TYPE

LEAF
ATTACHMENT

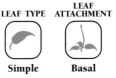

Regular

Simple

Basal

GIANT EVENING STAR
Mentzelia decapetala

Family: Stickleaf (Loasaceae)

Height: 12-32" (30-80 cm)

Flower: white, 4-5" (10-13 cm) wide, 10 lance-shaped petals surrounding a group of long, hair-like, yellow flower parts (stamens)

Leaf: lance-shaped, 4-10" (10-25 cm) long, sharply toothed and barbed, alternately attached

Bloom: summer

Cycle/Origin: perennial, native

Zone/Habitat: plains, foothills; dry slopes, canyon walls, roadsides

Range: eastern half of Colorado

Notes: During the day, Giant Evening Star looks similar to a thistle plant and may even be mistaken for a weed. As the common name suggests, the huge flowers open in the evening and remain so through the night; sometimes they can be spotted blooming in the early morning. Night-flying moths pollinate the flowers. Species name *decapetala* means "ten petals." Also known as Ten-petal Blazingstar or Moonflower.

FLOWER TYPE	LEAF TYPE	LEAF ATTACHMENT

Regular	Simple	Alternate

AMERICAN BISTORT
Polygonum bistortoides

Family: Buckwheat (Polygonaceae)

Height: 8-25" (20-63 cm)

Flower: dense elongated spike cluster, 1-2" (2.5-5 cm) long, made up of tiny individual white flowers with 5 petal-like sepals; cluster at end of erect reddish stalk

Leaf: grass-like, 6-10" (15-25 cm) long, with papery sheath at the node; leaves mostly basally attached, clasping the stem

Bloom: summer

Cycle/Origin: perennial, native

Zone/Habitat: montane, subalpine, alpine; open sites, meadows, moist hillsides, tundra

Range: western half of Colorado

Notes: A common summer wildflower in the mountains of Colorado. Thousands of American Bistort flowers and stalks will color meadows and tundra, waving gently in the wind. Also called Knotweed because, from a distance, the flower cluster looks like a knot on the long stalk. Once thought to cure snakebite, hence another common name, Snakeweed. Butterflies will feed on the nectar. Leaves can be eaten raw or cooked as greens. American Indians used the starchy roots for stews, soups and to make flour for bread.

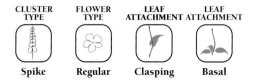

CLUSTER TYPE	FLOWER TYPE	LEAF ATTACHMENT	LEAF ATTACHMENT
Spike	Regular	Clasping	Basal

PEARLY EVERLASTING
Anaphalis margaritacea

Family: Aster (Asteraceae)

Height: 1-3' (30-90 cm)

Flower: round cluster, 1-2" (2.5-5 cm) wide, made of many individual white flower heads; individual flower, ¼" (.6 cm) long, composed of petal-like white bracts surrounding a yellow center (disk flowers)

Leaf: long and narrow, 3-5" (7.5-13 cm) long, greenish white; densely hairy underneath, causing it to look woolly white; alternately attached along the stem

Bloom: summer, fall

Cycle/Origin: perennial, native

Zone/Habitat: foothills, montane, subalpine; dry soils, pastures, along roads, fields, sun

Range: western half of Colorado

Notes: A common plant in the western half of Colorado, Pearly Everlasting blooms from summer to autumn. Its stems are covered with soft cottony hairs, and its flower clusters are often dried and used in floral arrangements. While it is the only species of its genus found in North America, individual plants can be highly variable. A host plant for American Painted Lady butterfly caterpillars, one of Colorado's overwintering adult butterflies. American Indians used the leaves as tobacco and as a treatment for throat problems and colds.

CLUSTER TYPE	FLOWER TYPE	LEAF TYPE	LEAF ATTACHMENT
Round	Composite	Simple	Alternate

SNOWBALL SAXIFRAGE
Saxifraga rhomboidea

Family: Saxifrage (Saxifragaceae)

Height: 6-12" (15-30 cm)

Flower: round cluster, 1-2½" (2.5-6 cm) wide, of white flowers; each flower, ¼-½" (.6-1 cm) wide, cup-shaped, made up of 5 rounded petals that surround a yellow center; cluster sits atop a leafless stalk

Leaf: diamond-shaped, 1-3" (2.5-7.5 cm) long, toothed, basally attached

Bloom: spring, summer

Cycle/Origin: perennial, native

Zone/Habitat: all life zones; moist hillsides, meadows, rocky slopes

Range: throughout

Notes: The leafless flower stalk of Snowball Saxifrage is a dead giveaway to identifying this plant. Also known as Diamondleaf Saxifrage because of the shape of the basal leaves. The flower stalk and clusters sway in the breeze, attracting insect pollinators. Can be found in all types of habitats in Colorado, but grows particularly well on open slopes in the foothills. Snowball Saxifrage growing in high elevations are smaller than those found in low altitudes.

CLUSTER TYPE	FLOWER TYPE	LEAF TYPE	LEAF ATTACHMENT

Round	Regular	Simple	Basal

ALPINE YARROW
Achillea millefolium alpicola

Family: Aster (Asteraceae)

Height: 6-10" (15-25 cm)

Flower: flat cluster, ½-3" (1-7.5 cm) wide, of dull white flowers; each flower, ⅙-¼" (.4-.6 cm) wide, has 5 petals (ray flowers) surrounding 20-30 light tan disk flowers

Leaf: fern-like, 3-5" (7.5-13 cm) long, divided into many tiny lobes, alternately attached

Bloom: summer

Cycle/Origin: perennial, native

Zone/Habitat: subalpine, alpine; open fields, in disturbed areas, tundra slopes

Range: western half of Colorado

Notes: Yarrow is an intensely studied group of plants whose medicinal qualities have been known for perhaps thousands of years. Genus name *Achillea* is from the Greek hero Achilles, who is said to have used yarrow on the battlefield to stop bleeding. Evidence does suggest that chemicals derived from this plant can reduce the clotting time of blood. A variety of and sometimes confused with Common Yarrow (pg. 257), which is more common, much taller, overall larger and found at lower elevations than Alpine Yarrow.

CLUSTER TYPE
Flat

FLOWER TYPE
Composite

LEAF TYPE
Simple Lobed

LEAF ATTACHMENT
Alternate

COWBANE
Oxypolis fendleri

Family: Carrot (Apiaceae)

Height: 18-30" (45-76 cm)

Flower: flat cluster, 2-3" (5-7.5 cm) wide, of tiny white flowers; individual flower has 5 petals

Leaf: compound, divided into 7 leaflets; each leaflet is lance-shaped, 2-3" (5-7.5 cm) long, and toothed

Bloom: summer

Cycle/Origin: perennial, native

Zone/Habitat: montane, subalpine; along streams, wet meadows

Range: western half of Colorado

Notes: Cowbane is so named because all of its plant parts are toxic to cattle, especially the roots. In spring, the plants pose a greater risk to cattle than in other times of the year, as the plants are small and the roots are easily pulled up and eaten. *Polis* in the genus name is from the Greek word for "white," and refers to the petals. This species is named after 1800s botanist Augustus Fendler.

CLUSTER TYPE	FLOWER TYPE	LEAF TYPE	LEAF ATTACHMENT
Flat	Regular	Compound	Alternate

CARAWAY
Carum carvi

Family: Carrot (Apiaceae)

Height: 2-3' (60-90 cm)

Flower: flat cluster, 2-3" (5-7.5) wide, of umbels formed by tiny white flowers; each flower, ¼" (.6 cm) wide

Leaf: compound, 3-10" (7.5-25 cm) long, divided into thin feathery leaflets; individual leaflet, 1-3" (2.5-7.5 cm) long; overall feathery appearance

Fruit: tiny round brown pod; contains 2 ridged, curved, dark brown seeds with pointed ends

Bloom: spring, summer

Cycle/Origin: biennial, non-native, introduced from western Asia

Zone/Habitat: foothills, montane; along roads, unused pastures, in fields

Range: western half of Colorado

Notes: Take great care when identifying the Caraway, as it looks similar to the toxic Poison Hemlock (pg. 269). Caraway has unspotted stems and feathery leaves, while Poison Hemlock has purple-spotted stems and fern-like leaves. Considered a noxious weed in Colorado. A common roadside plant that grows tall on curved stems with few leaves. Leaves can be eaten in salads or used to flavor soups. Edible seeds are high in protein and used to treat indigestion. Oil extracted from the seeds is used as a flavoring.

CLUSTER TYPE	FLOWER TYPE	LEAF TYPE	LEAF ATTACHMENT	LEAF ATTACHMENT	FRUIT
Flat	Regular	Compound	Alternate	Basal	Pod

COMMON YARROW
Achillea millefolium

Family: Aster (Asteraceae)

Height: 1-3' (30-90 cm)

Flower: tight flat-topped cluster, 2-4" (5-10 cm) wide, of white (sometimes pink) flowers; each tiny flower, ¼" (.6 cm) wide, has 4-6 (usually 5) petals

Leaf: fern-like, about 6" (15 cm) long, narrow, finely divided, feathery; leaves have a strong aroma and become progressively smaller toward the top; those at base are stalked, upper leaves are stalkless

Bloom: summer, fall

Cycle/Origin: perennial, native

Zone/Habitat: plains, foothills, montane; dry soils, forests, open fields, prairies, sun

Range: throughout

Notes: A common wildflower of open fields and along roads. A native of Eurasia as well as North America, it is uncertain which of our plants were introduced or are native. Often confused with a type of fern because of its leaves, this plant grows in large clusters due to a horizontal underground stem. Genus name *Achillea* comes from the legend that Achilles used the plant to treat bleeding wounds during the Trojan War. Species name *millefolium* means "thousand leaves," referring to the many divisions of the leaf, making one leaf look like many. Many cultures used it as a medicinal herb.

CLUSTER TYPE

Flat

FLOWER TYPE

Composite

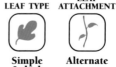

LEAF TYPE

Simple Lobed

LEAF ATTACHMENT

Alternate

BITTER CRESS
Cardamine cordifolia

Family: Mustard (Brassicaceae)

Height: 6-28" (15-71 cm)

Flower: open round cluster, 2-4" (5-10 cm) long, of white-to-off-white flowers; each flower, ½-¾" (1-2 cm) long, with 4 petals

Leaf: heart-shaped, 1-2" (2.5-5 cm) long, dark green, prominent veins, on a short stalk

Fruit: flat green seedpod, turning brown, ½" (1 cm) long

Bloom: summer

Cycle/Origin: perennial, native

Zone/Habitat: montane, subalpine; moist meadows, forest openings, stream banks

Range: western half of Colorado

Notes: Bitter Cress can be found in large patches when growing in its preferred moist conditions. Spreads by rhizomes and produces many leafy stems and flower clusters. Bitter Cress plants found growing in the subalpine zone look identical to those growing in the montane area, but are shorter. The leaves can be eaten raw, but taste bitter. Cooking the leaves will remove the bitterness and lend a peppery flavor when added to soups and stews.

CLUSTER TYPE	FLOWER TYPE	LEAF TYPE	LEAF ATTACHMENT	FRUIT
Round	Regular	Simple	Alternate	Pod

ALPINE THISTLE
Cirsium scopulorum

Family: Aster (Asteraceae)

Height: 1-2' (30-60 cm)

Flower: round cluster, 2-5" (5-13 cm) wide, of off-white to dirty white flowers; flowers hidden by bracts and dense cobweb-like hairs

Leaf: narrow and lobed, 4-7" (10-17.5 cm) long, tipped with very sharp spines, alternately attached

Bloom: summer, fall

Cycle/Origin: perennial, native

Zone/Habitat: subalpine, alpine; rocky hills, roadsides, disturbed areas

Range: western half of Colorado

Notes: A thistle native to Colorado, Alpine Thistle is also known as Frosty Ball because of its large hairy flower heads. Thistles are one type of plant that many people consider to be obnoxious weeds. However, many alpine plants (including Alpine Thistle) are useful in that they create small microclimates of warmer air, which insects use for warmth. Some American Indian tribes ate the roots of young plants after cooking them in a pit for several hours. Also called Mountain Thistle.

CLUSTER TYPE	FLOWER TYPE	LEAF TYPE	LEAF ATTACHMENT
Round	**Composite**	**Simple Lobed**	**Alternate**

ELEGANT DEATH CAMAS
Zigadenus elegans

Family: Lily (Liliaceae)

Height: 18-24" (45-60 cm)

Flower: very loose spike cluster, 2-5" (5-13 cm) long, of white-to-off-white flowers with light green centers; each flower, ¾" (2 cm) wide, made up of 6 fused petals that are actually 3 petals and 3 petal-like sepals; cluster at end of long leafless stem

Leaf: grass-like, 6-12" (15-30 cm) long, smooth, basally attached

Fruit: ovate green capsule, turning brown with age, ½-¾" (1-2 cm) long

Bloom: summer

Cycle/Origin: perennial, native

Zone/Habitat: all life zones except plains; moist sites, meadows, forest openings

Range: western half of Colorado

Notes: "Death" in the common name is a clue that people should stay clear of this plant. It is highly toxic–all plant parts contain the poisonous chemical zygadenine, which is more potent than strychnine. No part of this plant should ever be eaten. Responsible for many livestock deaths and the deaths of many early western settlers, who mistook the roots for edible onion or lily bulbs. Species name *elegans* is Latin for "elegant." Also called Mountain Death Camas.

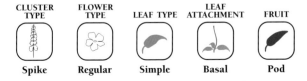

CLUSTER TYPE	FLOWER TYPE	LEAF TYPE	LEAF ATTACHMENT	FRUIT
Spike	Regular	Simple	Basal	Pod

COLORADO FALSE HELLEBORE
Veratrum tenuipetalum

Family: Lily (Liliaceae)

Height: 3-8' (90-240 cm)

Flower: spike cluster, 2-6" (5-15 cm) long, of whitish-to-light green flowers; each flower, ½-¾" (1-2 cm) wide, composed of 6 petal-like segments around a green center

Leaf: broadly oval, 8-14" (20-36 cm) long, alternately attached, clasping the stem; leaves are very large and have prominent parallel veins

Fruit: oval brown seed capsule, ¾-1¼" (2-3 cm) long

Bloom: summer

Cycle/Origin: perennial, native

Zone/Habitat: montane, subalpine; wet meadows, along streams, moist forests

Range: western half of Colorado

Notes: Unmistakable due its tall height, very leafy stems and huge leaves. Grows in large clumps in wet areas. Extremely poisonous to people and livestock. Ingesting only small amounts of the plant can be fatal to humans. Flowers are toxic to insects and may be responsible for losses in honeybee populations. American Indians traveled far to trade for plant parts to use for insect control; the plant is currently used by industry for insecticides. Also called Corn Lily, as it looks like a corn plant, or Skunk Cabbage, for its musky odor.

CLUSTER TYPE

Spike

FLOWER TYPE

Regular

LEAF TYPE

Simple

LEAF ATTACHMENT

Clasping

LEAF ATTACHMENT

Alternate

FRUIT

Pod

WHITE LOCOWEED
Oxytropis sericea

Family: Pea or Bean (Fabaceae)

Height: 6-18" (15-45 cm)

Flower: spike cluster, 2-6" (5-15 cm) long, of pea-like white flowers; each flower, ¾-1" (2-2.5 cm) long; cluster on a leafless stem begins at a height just above the basal leaves

Leaf: compound, 2-12" (5-30 cm) long, covered with tiny gray hairs, basally attached; each leaflet is lance-shaped, ½-1½" (1-4 cm) long

Fruit: ovate, light green pod; turning brown with age, ¼-½" (.6-1 cm) long

Bloom: spring, summer

Cycle/Origin: perennial, native

Zone/Habitat: all life zones except alpine; in meadows, gravelly slopes, fields and hillsides

Range: throughout

Notes: Also known as Rocky Mountain Loco or Silky Loco, White Locoweed blooms early in the spring, especially in the foothills. Hybridizes with Purple Locoweed (pg. 107), and the resulting plants produce flowers that may be light pink, cream or lavender. All locoweed are toxic and are responsible for many livestock deaths throughout the West. All are also poisonous to humans and should never be eaten.

CLUSTER TYPE	FLOWER TYPE	LEAF TYPE	LEAF ATTACHMENT	FRUIT
Spike	Irregular	Compound	Basal	Pod

POISON HEMLOCK
Conium maculatum

Family: Carrot (Apiaceae)

Height: 3-9' (90-270 cm)

Flower: large flat cluster, 2-6" (5-15 cm) wide, made of 12-15 umbels formed by tiny white flowers

Leaf: twice compound, divided into numerous sharply lobed and stalked leaflets; individual leaflet, 1-4" (2.5-10 cm) long, also divided numerous times and toothed; overall fern-like appearance

Fruit: ovate green seedpod, turning brown, less than ¼" (.6 cm) wide

Bloom: summer

Cycle/Origin: biennial, non-native, introduced from Europe

Zone/Habitat: plains, foothills; wet meadows, along streams, in ditches

Range: eastern half of Colorado

Notes: Poison Hemlock and many of its similar-looking relatives are deadly. Can be confused with Caraway (pg. 255) or Cow Parsnip (pg. 275). Look for the fern-like leaves and purple-spotted stems of Poison Hemlock to help identify. All of the plant parts are extremely toxic and ingesting only a small amount of this invasive weed can be fatal. Even using the hollow stem as a peashooter has lead to deaths. Was associated with Greek philosopher Socrates' death.

CLUSTER TYPE	FLOWER TYPE	LEAF TYPE	LEAF ATTACHMENT	LEAF ATTACHMENT	FRUIT
Flat	Regular	Twice Compound	Alternate	Basal	Pod

LOVAGE
Ligusticum porteri

Family: Carrot (Apiaceae)

Height: 20-36" (50-90 cm)

Flower: flat cluster, 2-8" (5-20 cm) wide, of small umbels formed by tiny white flowers; individual flower, ¼" (.5 cm) wide

Leaf: compound, 6-12" (15-30 cm) long, divided into 8-16 leaflets; individual leaflet, 2-3" (5-7.5 cm) long, coarsely toothed

Bloom: summer

Cycle/Origin: perennial, native

Zone/Habitat: foothills, montane, subalpine; in aspen groves and meadows

Range: western half of Colorado

Notes: Lovage is a common plant found growing in aspen groves of the Colorado mountains. A tall plant with reddish stems that are hollow and odorous. Leaves can be eaten and are used like celery. The roots have many medicinal uses such as treating fever, infection, toothache, headache–even tuberculosis. Some botanists fear that the popularity of the plant is leading to a decline in wild populations. Use extreme caution if using Lovage roots for medicine or food, as it resembles several species of deadly poisonous plants, including Poison Hemlock (pg. 269). Also called Porter Licorice Root.

CLUSTER TYPE	FLOWER TYPE	LEAF TYPE	LEAF ATTACHMENT	LEAF ATTACHMENT

Flat	Regular	Compound	Basal	Clasping

WHITE CLEMATIS
Clematis ligusticifolia

Family: Buttercup (Ranunculaceae)

Height: 3-30' (1-9.1 m); climbing vine

Flower: loose round cluster, 3-8" (7.5-20 cm) wide, of up to 20 white flowers; each flower, ½-¾" (1-2 cm) wide, made up of 5 petal-like sepals surrounding a group of yellow flower parts (stamens)

Leaf: compound, divided into 5-7 leaflets; each leaflet, 1-3" (2.5-7.5 cm) long, is triangular and toothed

Fruit: round, fuzzy, light green fruit; 1¼-2" (3-5 cm) wide; contains 1 seed with many long silky hairs; stays green well into fall

Bloom: spring, summer, early fall

Cycle/Origin: perennial, native

Zone/Habitat: plains, foothills; along streams, creeks and ravines

Range: eastern half of Colorado

Notes: A conspicuous vine in Colorado that sometimes nearly covers shrubs or trees. The fuzzy, ball-like fruit that appears in late summer and early fall makes identification of the vine unmistakable. Dioecious, with some plants producing only male flowers and others only female blooms. Often called Pepper Vine due to the peppery taste of the leaves, which American Indians chewed to relieve sore throats and cold symptoms. A tea made from the leaves constricts arteries in the brain and is used for migraine relief.

CLUSTER TYPE	FLOWER TYPE	LEAF TYPE	LEAF ATTACHMENT	FRUIT
Round	Regular	Compound	Opposite	Pod

COW PARSNIP
Heracleum maximum

Family: Carrot (Apiaceae)

Height: 4-9' (120-270 cm)

Flower: very large flat cluster, 4-8" (10-20 cm) wide, of white (sometimes purplish) flowers; individual flower, ½" (1 cm) wide, has notched petals and is often larger toward the outer edges of the cluster

Leaf: extremely large, up to 12" (30 cm) wide, often divided into 3 maple-leaf-like segments, 3-6" (7.5-15 cm) long, coarsely toothed; segments do not connect to one another and are often highly lobed; leafstalk is grossly swollen or inflated near the ridged and hollow main stem

Bloom: spring, summer

Cycle/Origin: perennial, native

Zone/Habitat: foothills, montane, subalpine; moist areas along roads, lakes and streams, sun

Range: western half of Colorado

Notes: Cow Parsnip is a very tall, single-stemmed plant with large leaves and flat clusters of white flowers. Do not confuse it with Poison Hemlock (pg. 269), which has fern-like compound leaves and purple-spotted stems. Look for the large inflated leafstalk (swelling) to help identify. The main stem is grooved and hollow. Commonly found growing in wet or moist soil. When the plant is bruised or cut, it emits a rancorous odor.

CLUSTER TYPE	FLOWER TYPE	LEAF TYPE	LEAF ATTACHMENT
Flat	**Regular**	**Simple Lobed**	**Alternate**

275

MINER'S CANDLE
Cryptantha virgata

Family: Borage (Boraginaceae)

Height: 10-24" (25-60 cm)

Flower: loose spike cluster, 4-12" (10-30 cm) long, of tiny white flowers; individual flower, ¼" (.6 cm) wide, has 5 petals surrounding a yellow center; flowers spaced around an unbranched stem

Leaf: narrow, 2-5" (5-13 cm) long, covered with stiff hairs; basally attached leaves are longer than upper (cauline) leaves

Bloom: spring, summer

Cycle/Origin: perennial or biennial, native

Zone/Habitat: plains, foothills, montane; dry meadows, fields, hillsides, canyons

Range: throughout

Notes: Miner's Candle grows as a biennial or perennial, depending on the weather or other conditions such as moisture content of the soil. The unbranched stem and narrow leaves are covered with stiff hairs, making them prickly to the touch. Leaves near the top of the stem protrude from among the tiny white flowers. The dried stems stand well into winter and provide seeds for songbirds. Species name *virgata* comes from the Greek words for "mountain" and "nut," and refers to its habitat and nut-like seeds.

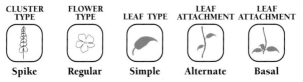

CLUSTER TYPE	FLOWER TYPE	LEAF TYPE	LEAF ATTACHMENT	LEAF ATTACHMENT
Spike	Regular	Simple	Alternate	Basal

SOAPWEED YUCCA
Yucca glauca

Family: Agave (Agavaceae)

Height: 2-3' (60-90 cm); shrub

Flower: tall spike cluster, 5-15" (13-38 cm) long, of ovate, creamy-to-greenish white flowers; each nodding flower, 2-3" (5-7.5 cm) wide, 3 petals and 3 petal-like sepals; on a stalk, 3-6' (90-180 cm) long

Leaf: lance-shaped, 8-36" (20-90 cm) long, rigid, sharp-tipped, margins frayed with thread-like filaments

Fruit: large brown seed capsule, 2-3" (5-7.5 cm) long, 6 vertical segments, splits open at the top at maturity

Bloom: spring, summer

Cycle/Origin: perennial, native

Zone/Habitat: plains, foothills; deserts, prairies, rocky slopes

Range: eastern half of Colorado

Notes: Soapweed Yucca sometimes dominates miles of open areas. Flowers open fully only at night and have a mutually beneficial relationship with Yucca Moths. The female pollinates a flower and deposits her egg in the same visit. Resulting larva feeds on seeds, then eats its way out of the pod. This relationship ensures fertilized yucca flowers and well-fed Yucca Moth larvae. The Navajo Indians relied heavily on yucca–roots were pounded to make a soapy substance for cleaning; leaves were used for all-purpose ties, sandals and mats; and petals and pods were eaten.

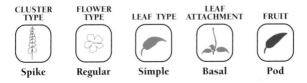

CLUSTER TYPE	FLOWER TYPE	LEAF TYPE	LEAF ATTACHMENT	FRUIT
Spike	Regular	Simple	Basal	Pod

ROCKY MOUNTAIN CINQUEFOIL
Potentilla rubricaulis

Family: Rose (Rosaceae)

Height: 12-18" (30-45 cm)

Flower: pale yellow, ½" (1 cm) wide, with 5 rounded petals surrounding yellow flower parts (stamens); flowers found in groups

Leaf: compound, divided into several stalks and as many as 15 leaflets; each leaflet, 1-2" (2.5-5 cm) long, has numerous lobes

Bloom: spring, summer

Cycle/Origin: perennial, native

Zone/Habitat: all life zones except alpine; dry meadows, slopes

Range: throughout

Notes: The cinquefoil species most commonly seen in the Colorado plains. Rocky Mountain Cinquefoil growing in the plains will bloom a bit earlier than cinquefoils in higher elevations. The leaves and stems of this plant are often so hairy that they look woolly. Plains Indian tribes cooked and consumed the woody root. Makes a good addition to rock gardens, as it is heat and drought tolerant.

FLOWER TYPE — Regular   LEAF TYPE — Compound   LEAF ATTACHMENT — Alternate

WESTERN HAWKSBEARD
Crepis occidentalis

Family: Aster (Asteraceae)

Height: 6-18" (15-45 cm)

Flower: yellow, ½" (1 cm) wide, composed of ray flowers only; wiry stem branches near the top and supports several flowers

Leaf: deeply lobed, 4-10" (10-25 cm) long, grayish green, sticky, basally attached

Bloom: spring, summer

Cycle/Origin: perennial, native

Zone/Habitat: plains, foothills; dry slopes and hillsides, prairies

Range: eastern half of Colorado

Notes: Western Hawksbeard blooms in early spring in eastern Colorado, especially on sunny, south-facing slopes of the foothills. Produces flowers that attract insects, but actual pollination is rare. Instead, it usually produces seeds without fertilization, which results in genetically identical individual plants. The leaves look somewhat similar to those of Common Dandelion (pg. 317), but can be differentiated from them by one touch of the thick sticky leaves. Also called Large-flowered Hawksbeard.

FLOWER TYPE

LEAF TYPE

LEAF ATTACHMENT

Composite

Simple Lobed

Basal

PRICKLY LETTUCE
Lactuca serriola

Family: Aster (Asteraceae)

Height: 12-40" (30-102 cm)

Flower: pale yellow, ½-¾" (1-2 cm) wide, composed of square-tipped, fringed ray flowers only

Leaf: lobed, 2-4" (5-10 cm) long, deeply lobed, light green with sharp cactus-like spines along the edges, alternately attached

Bloom: summer, fall

Cycle/Origin: annual, non-native

Zone/Habitat: plains, foothills; in dry fields and disturbed sites, along roads

Range: eastern half of Colorado

Notes: Prickly Lettuce was introduced from Europe and is now classified in Colorado as a noxious weed. Many county governments have plans in place to stop the spread of this plant. Its spiny leaves make eradication tough work for gardeners. The young leaves are edible, but the older leaves are not since they are prickly like a cactus. Multi-branched woody stem produces many small yellow flowers. When broken, the foliage exudes lots of milky sap, which is used medicinally as an ingredient in sedatives to treat insomnia. Oil from the seeds is used for making soap and paint.

FLOWER TYPE

Composite

LEAF TYPE

Simple Lobed

LEAF ATTACHMENT

Alternate

COLORADO GUMWEED
Grindelia inornata

Family: Aster (Asteraceae)

Height: 1-2' (30-60 cm)

Flower: yellow, ½-1" (1-2.5 cm) wide, round, made up of only disk flowers (lacking ray flowers); overlapping, down-curved, fleshy green bracts

Leaf: elongated oval, 4-10" (10-25 cm) long, thick with finely toothed edges, alternately attached; lower leaves are on stalks, upper leaves clasp the stem

Bloom: summer, fall

Cycle/Origin: perennial, native

Zone/Habitat: plains; hillsides, fields

Range: eastern half of Colorado

Notes: The Colorado Gumweed is easy to distinguish from other gumweeds because it is made up entirely of disk flowers, lacking ray flowers. This is a plant of lower elevations in Colorado, and while not as common as the Curlycup Gumweed (pg. 297), it can still be found throughout much of the eastern half of the state. Gumweeds get their common name from the sticky resin that coats the upper portion of the plant. While several gumweed species do have medicinal qualities, the plant can be toxic to livestock. The level of toxicity depends upon the soil content in which they grow. If the element selenium is present, the roots absorb it and the plants become poisonous.

FLOWER TYPE   LEAF TYPE   LEAF ATTACHMENT   LEAF ATTACHMENT

Composite   Simple   Alternate

Clasping

ALPINE AVENS
Geum rossii

Family: Rose (Rosaceae)

Height: 6-12" (15-30 cm)

Flower: shiny yellow, ¾" (2 cm) wide, made of 5 rounded petals and 5 petal-like green sepals surrounding a feathery yellow center

Leaf: mainly compound (a few lobed), 4-6" (10-15 cm) long, composed of fine-toothed leaflets; each leaflet, ½" (1 cm) long, dark green and covered with fine hairs; leaves are basally attached

Fruit: round bur-like seed head, ½-¾" (1-2 cm) wide; seeds have feathery tips that turn prickly and hooked with age

Bloom: summer

Cycle/Origin: perennial, native

Zone/Habitat: subalpine, alpine; tundra meadows, talus slopes, alpine boulder fields, roadsides

Range: western half of Colorado

Notes: Often found in large patches, coloring entire hillsides yellow. Bur-like fruit of Alpine Avens is feathery, turning prickly with tiny hooked bristles when mature. The bristles catch on fur or clothing, thus easily dispersing the seeds. American Indians called it Jealousy Plant, believing the fruit was trying to harm passersby as if envious of their mobility. Also called Ross Avens after botanist James Ross.

FLOWER TYPE	LEAF TYPE	LEAF ATTACHMENT	FRUIT
Regular	Compound	Basal	Pod

289

YELLOW PRAIRIE VIOLET
Viola nuttallii

Family: Violet (Violaceae)

Height: 4-8" (10-20 cm)

Flower: bright yellow, ¾" (2 cm) wide, made up 2 backward-curved upper petals and 3 lower petals and a hairy, black-striped throat

Leaf: lance-shaped, 3-8" (7.5-20 cm) long, dark green, stalked, basally attached

Bloom: spring, summer

Cycle/Origin: perennial, native

Zone/Habitat: all life zones except alpine; open hillsides, in fields and prairies

Range: throughout

Notes: Yellow Prairie Violet is the most common violet in Colorado, growing in all habitats except the alpine zone. Its bright yellow flowers nod from the top of leafless stalks. The leaves can be eaten raw or cooked and are high in vitamins A and C. However, the roots and seeds should never be eaten, as they can cause severe stomach problems. This plant is also called Nuttall Violet or Wild Pansy.

FLOWER TYPE	LEAF TYPE	LEAF ATTACHMENT

Irregular	**Simple**	**Basal**

CUTLEAF CONEFLOWER
Rudbeckia laciniata

Family: Aster (Asteraceae)

Height: 5-8' (150-240 cm)

Flower: yellow, ¾-1" (2-2.5 cm) tall, composed of a cone-shaped green center (disk flowers) surrounded by 8-10 drooping petals (ray flowers); each plant grows 20-50 large composite flower heads

Leaf: lobed lower, 5-8" (13-20 cm) long, 3-5 sharp lobes, coarse teeth; simple upper, 2-3" (5-7.5 cm) long, coarsely toothed, nearly clasping the stem

Bloom: summer, fall

Cycle/Origin: perennial, native

Zone/Habitat: foothills, montane; wet soils, fields, ditches, prairies

Range: western half of Colorado

Notes: A tall robust perennial, the Cutleaf Coneflower grows in moist soils in western Colorado. Look for its green center (cone) and drooping yellow petals, along with the lobed lower leaves and simple upper leaves, to help identify. Often seen growing in ditches or along roads and near old homesteads, it is also called Golden Glow. A good plant for a butterfly garden. Its flowers attract butterflies such as the Monarch to feed on the nectar. Also known as Green-headed Coneflower.

FLOWER TYPE	LEAF TYPE	LEAF TYPE	LEAF ATTACHMENT
Composite	Simple	Simple Lobed	Alternate

ROCKYSCREE FALSE GOLDEN-ASTER
Heterotheca fulcrata

Family: Aster (Asteraceae)

Height: 10-24" (25-60 cm)

Flower: yellow, 1" (2.5 cm) wide, with 10-25 thin petals (ray flowers) surrounding a yellow center (disk flowers); single (or multiple) flowers sit atop reddish stems

Leaf: lance-shaped, up to 2" (5 cm) long, covered with white hairs, alternately attached

Bloom: summer

Cycle/Origin: perennial, native

Zone/Habitat: montane, subalpine; dry hillsides, meadows, forest openings

Range: western half of Colorado

Notes: Rockyscree False Golden-aster has reddish stems that give rise to a single or several flower heads. Look for the hairy leaves with bristly edges to help identify this plant. The genus name *Heterotheca* is Greek, with *Hetero* for "different" and *theca* for "case," referring to the ray and disk flowers producing differing seeds (unlike the identical seeds other asters produce). American Indians used the roots of this plant to relieve toothaches. There are several subspecies of Rockyscree False Golden-aster, with subtle differences among them.

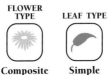

FLOWER TYPE — LEAF TYPE

Composite — **Simple**

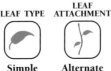

LEAF ATTACHMENT

Alternate

CURLYCUP GUMWEED
Grindelia squarrosa

Family: Aster (Asteraceae)

Height: 6-36" (15-90 cm)

Flower: yellow, 1" (2.5 cm) wide, with 20 or more short petals (ray flowers) surrounding a central yellow disk (disk flowers); 3-20 flower heads; outward-curling green bracts surround each head; glands on bracts exude a sticky gum-like resin

Leaf: oval, 1-2½" (2.5-6 cm) long, often wavy or curled edges and coarse teeth, usually lacking a leafstalk

Bloom: summer, fall

Cycle/Origin: perennial, native

Zone/Habitat: plains, foothills; dry or disturbed soils, fields, along roads, sun

Range: eastern half of Colorado

Notes: Also called Gum Plant, Sticky Heads or Tarweed, its many common names refer to the sticky resin secreted from glands on bracts that surround each flower head. Gumweed resin will stain your hands and has been used by many cultures as a medicine for everything from asthma to healing wounds. A native plant of the American West. One of the first plants to grow after construction or in heavily grazed fields and is commonly seen along roads and railroads. Its flower heads are frequently used in arrangements of dried flowers.

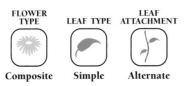

FLOWER TYPE	LEAF TYPE	LEAF ATTACHMENT
Composite	Simple	Alternate

ALPINE GOLDENWEED
Tonestus lyallii

Family: Aster (Asteraceae)

Height: 2-6" (5-15 cm)

Flower: yellow, 1" (2.5 cm) wide, composed of 15-30 petals (ray flowers) surrounding a yellow cluster of raised disk flowers

Leaf: elongated spoon-shaped, up to 3" (7.5 cm) long, covered with short dense hairs, alternately attached

Bloom: summer, fall

Cycle/Origin: perennial, native

Zone/Habitat: alpine; rocky ridges, tundra slopes

Range: western half of Colorado

Notes: Alpine Goldenweed reproduces by seed, but also spreads by stems (rhizomes) that work their way under and around rocks. Like most alpine plants, it sprouts quickly once the winter snow disappears and stores much of its energy in a taproot. The flowers look similar to those of Broadleaf Arnica (pg. 311), but the plants can be distinguished from each other by the leaves. Alpine Goldenweed has alternately attached leaves, while the leaves of Broadleaf Arnica are oppositely attached. Attracts flies, bees and high altitude butterflies as pollinators. This plant was named by British botanist David Lyall and is also known as Lyall Goldenweed.

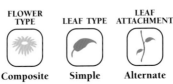

FLOWER TYPE — Composite
LEAF TYPE — Simple
LEAF ATTACHMENT — Alternate

HEARTLEAF BUTTERCUP
Ranunculus cardiophyllus

Family: Buttercup (Ranunculaceae)

Height: 6-12" (15-30 cm)

Flower: glossy yellow, 1" (2.5 cm) wide, cup-shaped, made up of 5 petals and 5 hairy petal-like sepals

Leaf: roughly heart-shaped, 1-2" (2.5-5 cm) wide, basally attached; stem (cauline) has 3-5 deep lobes and is alternately attached; both types are hairy

Bloom: summer

Cycle/Origin: perennial, native

Zone/Habitat: montane, subalpine, alpine; moist areas near ponds, along streams

Range: western half of Colorado

Notes: The sap of all buttercups is mildly toxic to skin and very toxic to mucus membranes of the nose and mouth; intense pain and blistering can result from contact. Please use caution if holding buttercups under the chin to determine whether one likes butter (according to the old wives' tale), as some people with sensitive skin can get a rash by merely touching the plant. Heartleaf Buttercup can be distinguished from other buttercups by the heart-shaped basal and the deeply lobed stem leaves. *Cardio* in the species name is Greek and means "pertaining to the heart," referring to the shape of the leaves.

FLOWER TYPE	LEAF TYPE	LEAF ATTACHMENT	LEAF ATTACHMENT
Regular	Simple Lobed	Alternate	Basal

LEAFY CINQUEFOIL
Potentilla fissa

Family: Rose (Rosaceae)

Height: 6-12" (15-30 cm)

Flower: yellow (rarely off-white), 1" (2.5 cm) wide, with 5 rounded petals surrounding yellow flower parts (stamens); flowers found in groups

Leaf: compound, divided into as many as 13 leaflets; each leaflet, 1-3" (2.5-7.5 cm) long, toothed, hairy

Bloom: spring, summer

Cycle/Origin: perennial, native

Zone/Habitat: foothills, montane, subalpine; meadows, forest openings, along roads, and rocky slopes

Range: western half of Colorado

Notes: Hikers in the Colorado mountains are sure to spot cinquefoils along most routes, but identification is often a challenge. Leafy Cinquefoil is one of the most commonly seen plants with five-petaled yellow flowers in Colorado and can be distinguished from other cinquefoils by the large size and amount of leaves. The genus name *Potentilla* comes from the Latin word for "potent," and refers to the way these plants can control bleeding. A host plant for several species of Copper butterflies.

FLOWER TYPE

Regular

LEAF TYPE

Compound

LEAF ATTACHMENT

Alternate

LEAF ATTACHMENT

Basal

SHRUBBY CINQUEFOIL
Dasiphora fruticosa

Family: Rose (Rosaceae)

Height: 15-40" (38-102 cm); shrub

Flower: bright yellow, 1-1½" (2.5-4 cm) wide, 5 rounded petals surrounding yellow flower parts (stamens)

Leaf: compound, divided into several stalks and as many as 7 (usually 5) leaflets; each leaflet, 1" (2.5 cm) long, is gray and hairy

Bloom: summer, fall

Cycle/Origin: perennial, native

Zone/Habitat: all life zones except plains; open forests, ridges

Range: western half of Colorado

Notes: It is easy to distinguish Shrubby Cinquefoil from other cinquefoils by its overall rounded shape. Also called Yellow Rose, this shrub is easily cultivated and very popular among landscapers in the West. The blooms persist for as long as four months, which is one reason it is popular in gardens. Some varieties have been bred to produce unusually large flowers. A host plant for the Dorcas Copper butterfly.

FLOWER TYPE

Regular

LEAF TYPE

Compound

LEAF ATTACHMENT

Alternate

YELLOW MONKEYFLOWER
Mimulus guttatus

Family: Snapdragon (Scrophulariaceae)

Height: 1-2' (30-60 cm)

Flower: yellow, 1-1½" (2.5-4 cm) long, 2 petals (lips) fuse together to form a tube; upper lip has 2 lobes bent upward, lower lip has 3 lobes bent downward; lower lip sometimes has red spots near the throat

Leaf: oval, 1-3" (2.5-7.5 cm) long, sharp-toothed edges, oppositely attached

Fruit: green pod, turning brown, ½-¾" (1-2 cm) long; looks like an inflated balloon

Bloom: spring, summer

Cycle/Origin: perennial, native

Zone/Habitat: foothills, montane, subalpine; wet areas, springs, seeps, along lakes and ponds

Range: western half of Colorado

Notes: Yellow Monkeyflowers can be highly variable; sometimes the plants are small and grow singly, other times they grow bushy and in groups. The flower prevents self-pollination in a unique way. Its two-part stigma is initially open, but will immediately close when a pollen-carrying insect brushes up against it. Thus it holds the pollen from the insect firmly and prevents its own pollen from making contact with the stigma. Also called Seep Monkeyflower.

FLOWER TYPE	LEAF TYPE	LEAF ATTACHMENT	FRUIT
Irregular	**Simple**	**Opposite**	**Pod**

PLAINS ZINNIA
Zinnia grandiflora

Family: Aster (Asteraceae)

Height: 4-8" (10-20 cm)

Flower: bright yellow (sometimes orange-yellow), 1-1½" (2.5-4 cm) wide, composed of 3-6 round petals (ray flowers) surrounding a small group of orange or reddish disk flowers

Leaf: narrow, 1-2" (2.5-5 cm) long, oppositely attached

Bloom: summer, fall

Cycle/Origin: perennial, native

Zone/Habitat: plains; deserts, rocky slopes

Range: eastern half of Colorado

Notes: Plains Zinnia grows in clumps, and during a good growing season, the flowers can dot southeastern Colorado deserts with beautiful yellow color. The petals turn papery with age, giving this plant one of its other common names, Golden Paperflower. The genus *Zinnia* is named after German botanist Johann Zinn, who collected seeds of a similar plant in Mexico from which the garden variety of zinnia is descended. This plant is also known as Little Golden Zinnia.

FLOWER TYPE

Composite

LEAF TYPE

Simple

LEAF ATTACHMENT

Opposite

BROADLEAF ARNICA
Arnica latifolia

Family: Aster (Asteraceae)

Height: 4-12" (10-30 cm)

Flower: yellow, 1-1½" (2.5-4 cm) wide, made up of 8-16 petals (ray flowers) and many darker yellow disk flowers; usually a single flower (sometimes 2 or 3)

Leaf: broadly triangular, up to 2" (5 cm) long, coarsely toothed, oppositely attached

Bloom: summer

Cycle/Origin: perennial, native

Zone/Habitat: montane, subalpine; moist areas, forests

Range: western half of Colorado

Notes: At first glance, this plant looks similar to Heartleaf Arnica (pg. 341), but further inspection of the leaves will help distinguish between the two. Broadleaf Arnica leaves are half the size as those of Heartleaf Arnica and rarely heart-shaped. Usually seen growing in dense clumps with protruding single flower stems. Widely spreads by horizontal underground stems (rhizomes). American Indians used the leaves of this plant as a poultice to help heal cuts and bruises.

FLOWER TYPE	**LEAF TYPE**	**LEAF ATTACHMENT**
Composite	Simple	Opposite

DWARF MOUNTAIN RAGWORT
Senecio fremontii

Family: Aster (Asteraceae)

Height: 6-18" (15-45 cm)

Flower: yellow, 1-1½" (2.5-4 cm) wide, made up of 8-15 petals (ray flowers) surrounding a flat yellow center (disk flowers)

Leaf: oval, 2" (5 cm) long, thick, toothed, hairless, alternately attached; leaves are mostly along the stem, the few basal leaves are small and inconspicuous

Bloom: summer

Cycle/Origin: perennial, native

Zone/Habitat: subalpine, alpine; rocky slopes, talus fields

Range: western half of Colorado

Notes: Considering the habitat and life zone will help identify Dwarf Mountain Ragwort, in addition to looking for the oval leaves. This plant grows in areas where fertile soil is rare and in which it is tough to survive, such as on rocky slopes and in talus fields. Individual plants growing above the timberline will be much smaller than those growing at lower elevations. A member of the *Senecio* genus, which is one of the most common and numerous of the flowering plant genera with over 2,000 species worldwide. Also called Rock Ragwort.

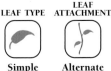

FLOWER TYPE	LEAF TYPE	LEAF ATTACHMENT
Composite	Simple	Alternate

SUBALPINE GUMWEED
Grindelia subalpina

Family: Aster (Asteraceae)

Height: 12-18" (30-45 cm)

Flower: yellow, 1-1¾" (2.5-4.5 cm) wide, made up of stiff yellow petals (ray flowers) surrounding a yellow disk; sticky recurved green or reddish bracts

Leaf: elongated, 1-4" (2.5-10 cm) long, coarse-toothed margins, covered with hairs, basally and alternately attached

Bloom: late summer

Cycle/Origin: perennial, native

Zone/Habitat: montane, subalpine; in disturbed soils, in fields, along roads

Range: western half of Colorado

Notes: Very similar looking to Curlycup Gumweed (pg. 297), but has larger flowers and leaves. Note the elevation in which you find your wildflower–Subalpine grows in higher altitudes than Curlycup. The stems branch often and give rise to many flower heads. American Indians used the plant for many purposes. They chewed the leaves like a gum and used the leaves for a tea-like drink. The flower heads were ground to a pulp and used as a salve to relieve the itch of poison ivy and to treat coughs and congestion. Gumweed is still used today in asthma treatments.

FLOWER TYPE	LEAF TYPE	LEAF ATTACHMENT	LEAF ATTACHMENT

Composite	**Simple**	**Alternate**	**Basal**

COMMON DANDELION
Taraxacum officinale

Family: Aster (Asteraceae)

Height: 2-18" (5-45 cm)

Flower: yellow, 1½" (4 cm) wide; appears as 1 large flower, but is actually a composite of many tiny flowers that are clustered together

Leaf: lobed, 2-8" (5-20 cm) long, with deep lobes and sharp teeth, basally attached

Bloom: spring, summer, fall

Cycle/Origin: perennial, non-native

Zone/Habitat: all life zones; dry soils, lawns, fields, sun

Range: throughout

Notes: A non-native perennial responsible for much water contamination, as people treat lawns with chemicals to eradicate Common Dandelion. In French, *dent-de-lion* refers to the toothed leaves, which resemble the teeth of a lion. Its flowers open in mornings and close in afternoons. The globe-like seed heads have soft hair-like bristles that resemble tiny parachutes, which carry the seeds away on the wind. Originally brought from Eurasia as a food crop. Its leaves are bitter, but offer high vitamin and mineral content. The long taproot can be roasted and ground to use as a coffee substitute.

FLOWER TYPE	LEAF TYPE	LEAF ATTACHMENT
Composite	Simple Lobed	Basal

STEMLESS FOUR-NERVE DAISY
Tetraneuris acaulis

Family: Aster (Asteraceae)

Height: 4-10" (10-25 cm)

Flower: yellow, 1-2" (2.5-5 cm) wide, made up of 10-20 petals (ray flowers) with irregular tooth-like edges surrounding a raised yellow center (disk flowers)

Leaf: elongated, 1-3" (2.5-7.5 cm) long, hairy or smooth, basally attached

Bloom: summer

Cycle/Origin: perennial, native

Zone/Habitat: alpine; dry soils, open hillsides, rocky ridges

Range: western half of Colorado

Notes: Stemless Four-nerve Daisy flowers have a similar shape as those of the Alpine Sunflower (pg. 347), but are half the size. The texture of the stems and leaves is highly variable–some plants will have smooth stalks and foliage, while others nearby will be very hairy. This plant stores much energy in its huge taproot due to the short alpine growing season. Pollinated chiefly by butterflies and bees. Flowers are short-lived and turn quickly to seed. Also known as Woolly Actinella, Stemless Hymenoxys or Butte Marigold.

FLOWER TYPE	LEAF TYPE	LEAF ATTACHMENT

Composite	Simple	Basal

COWPEN DAISY
Verbesina encelioides

Family: Aster (Asteraceae)

Height: 1-2' (30-60 cm)

Flower: bright yellow, 1-2" (2.5-5 cm) wide, composed of 5-10 notched petals (ray flowers) surrounding a light orange center (disk flowers)

Leaf: broad, nearly triangular, 2-4" (5-10 cm) long, coarsely toothed edges, oppositely attached along a hairy stem

Bloom: summer, early fall

Cycle/Origin: annual, native

Zone/Habitat: plains, foothills; disturbed soils, roadsides, pastures

Range: eastern half of Colorado

Notes: Cowpen Daisies sometimes bloom abundantly, coloring miles of Colorado roadsides or pastures a solid yellow. Main stem is hairy and branches into many stems, which support several flowers. The flowers are showy, but have a rancorous aroma. Bees and butterflies commonly pollinate the flowers and apparently do not mind the foul odor. American Indians used the plant to treat skin ailments. Also known as Golden Crownbeard or Goldweed.

FLOWER TYPE	LEAF TYPE	LEAF ATTACHMENT
Composite	Simple	Opposite

GOLDENEYE
Heliomeris multiflora

Family: Aster (Asteraceae)

Height: 2-4' (60-120 cm)

Flower: yellow, 1-2" (2.5-5 cm) wide, composed of 10-15 wide petals (ray flowers) surrounding a slightly raised yellow or orange center (disk flowers)

Leaf: lance-shaped, 2-4" (5-10 cm) long, rough to the touch, oppositely attached

Bloom: late summer

Cycle/Origin: perennial, native

Zone/Habitat: foothills, montane; along roads, hillsides, dry forest openings

Range: western half of Colorado

Notes: One of the most common yellow roadside flowers in the Colorado foothills. The many branching stems give rise to many flowers, which resemble small sunflowers. Look for oppositely attached leaves that are rough to the touch and the wiry bristly stems to help identify. *Helio* in the genus name is the Greek word for "sun," and is a reason for another common name, Sunspots. A host plant for some crescentspot and patch butterflies.

FLOWER TYPE	LEAF TYPE	LEAF ATTACHMENT
Composite	Simple	Opposite

HAIRY EVENING-PRIMROSE
Oenothera villosa

Family: Evening-primrose (Onagraceae)

Height: 2-4' (60-120 cm)

Flower: bright yellow, 1-2" (2.5-5 cm) wide, 4 petals; in groups atop hairy stems

Leaf: lance-shaped, 4-8" (10-20 cm) long, hairy, alternately attached; sometimes with fine teeth

Fruit: pod-like green container, turning brown with age, ½-2" (1-5 cm) long

Bloom: summer, fall

Cycle/Origin: biennial, native

Zone/Habitat: plains, foothills; along roads and farm fences, open disturbed fields

Range: eastern half of Colorado

Notes: Hairy Evening-primrose is a true biennial, producing a low rosette of leaves the first year and a tall flowering stalk the next. The flowers are fleeting; they open during evenings in summer and wilt by noon the following day. Moths pollinate the flowers at night. The leaves can be cooked and eaten as greens, but taste quite bitter. American Indians used a mixture of the roots and honey for a cough syrup. This species has many other common names such as Yellow, Hooker, Showy or Erect Evening-primrose.

FLOWER TYPE	LEAF TYPE	LEAF ATTACHMENT	LEAF ATTACHMENT	FRUIT
Regular	Simple	Alternate	Basal	Pod

GOLDEN EVENING-PRIMROSE
Oenothera howardii

Family: Evening-primrose (Onagraceae)

Height: 1-2' (30-60 cm)

Flower: bright yellow, 1½-2½" (4-6 cm) wide, made up of 4 petals that fuse together to form a long tube; sits atop a flower stalk

Leaf: lance-shaped, 2-6" (5-15 cm) long, on a short leaf-stalk, basally and alternately attached

Bloom: spring, summer

Cycle/Origin: perennial, native

Zone/Habitat: plains, foothills; dry slopes, along roads

Range: eastern half of Colorado

Notes: Evening-primroses are so named because the flowers open late in the day, stay open overnight and wilt by noon the following day. The Evening-primrose family encompasses about 675 species worldwide. Plants in this family are not related to true primroses such as Fairy Primrose (pg. 65) or Parry Primrose, (pg. 67), but were named "primrose" by a botanist in the early 1600s. The height of Golden Evening-primrose is highly variable. Its flowers are pollinated at night, chiefly by moths. All parts of the plant are edible—the roots have a delicious peppery taste. Roots and shoots have been used for treating eczema, headache and asthma. Known by at least two other common names over the years, including Howard Evening-primrose and Yellow Stemless Evening-primrose.

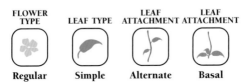

FLOWER TYPE	LEAF TYPE	LEAF ATTACHMENT	LEAF ATTACHMENT
Regular	Simple	Alternate	Basal

YELLOW AVALANCHE LILY
Erythronium grandiflorum

Family: Lily (Liliaceae)

Height: 6-12" (15-30 cm)

Flower: bright yellow, 1¼-2½" (3-6 cm) wide, 6 backward-curving petals (actually 3 petals and 3 petal-like sepals), large plant parts protruding beyond the petals; 1-3 hanging flowers per stalk

Leaf: broadly lance-shaped, up to 8" (20 cm) long, basally attached; 2 leaves per plant

Fruit: 3-sided green capsule, turning brown with age, 1¼-1½" (3-4 cm) long

Bloom: spring, summer

Cycle/Origin: perennial, native

Zone/Habitat: montane, subalpine, alpine; wet areas, snow banks, meadows near aspen groves, damp forest openings

Range: western half of Colorado

Notes: A beautiful wildflower, Yellow Avalanche Lily grows near the snow line and blooms when the snow begins to melt. Also known as Snow Lily or Glacier Lily. May take four or more years to flower, so please do not pick, try to transplant or trample this plant. The flowers are pollinated by insects. American Indians harvested the bulbs in the springtime for food.

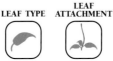

FLOWER TYPE	LEAF TYPE	LEAF ATTACHMENT	FRUIT
Bell	Simple	Basal	Pod

PRAIRIE CONEFLOWER
Ratibida columnifera

Family: Aster (Asteraceae)

Height: 12-30" (30-76 cm)

Flower: yellow to dark red (sometimes has both colors), 1-3" (2.5-7.5 cm) tall, made up of a cone-shaped, yellow-to-brown center, ½-2" (1-5 cm) tall, of tiny disk flowers surrounded by 4-8 drooping petals (ray flowers), ½-¾" (1-2 cm) long

Leaf: lobed, 3-6" (7.5-15 cm) long, hairy with deep lobes; each lobe, 1-3" (2.5-7.5 cm) long

Fruit: conical light brown seedpod, 1-3" (2.5-7.5 cm) long

Bloom: summer

Cycle/Origin: perennial, native

Zone/Habitat: plains, foothills; disturbed areas, along roads, on hillsides, mesas, sunny slopes

Range: eastern half of Colorado

Notes: The brown center of Prairie Coneflower protrudes from the surrounding drooping colorful rays. Also known as Mexican Hat because the flower head resembles the traditional broad-brimmed, high-centered hat worn during Mexican fiestas. Drought tolerant and shade intolerant. In summer, sunny fields are awash with color by thousands of Prairie Coneflower blooms. Flower heads attract many types of insects and are a good nectar source for butterflies. The leaves and flower heads can be used to make a tea.

FLOWER TYPE	LEAF TYPE	LEAF ATTACHMENT	FRUIT
Composite	Simple Lobed	Alternate	Pod

GOAT'S BEARD
Tragopogon dubius

Family: Aster (Asteraceae)

Height: 1-3' (30-90 cm)

Flower: yellow, 2-2½" (5-6 cm) wide, large and dandelion-like, composed of many petals (ray flowers), but no center disk flowers; stalk is swollen just below the flower head

Leaf: grass-like, 12" (30 cm) long and just ½" (1 cm) wide, alternately attached, clasping the stem

Bloom: spring, summer

Cycle/Origin: biennial or perennial, non-native

Zone/Habitat: plains, foothills, montane; dry soils, open fields, along roads, sun

Range: throughout

Notes: Sometimes called Yellow Salsify, this European import looks like a large dandelion and is common along roads and in open fields. Its large yellow flower head, which turns to face the sun, opens only on sunny mornings and closes by noon, which has led to another common name, Johnny-go-to-bed-at-noon (several other plants share this moniker). The entire plant produces a sticky, milky sap. Its long taproots can be dug up, roasted and ground to be used as a coffee substitute. The seed head looks like a giant dandelion plume or like an old gray goat's beard, and children often refer to its mature flower heads as blow balls. Some people spray these seed heads with hairspray and use them in dried flower arrangements.

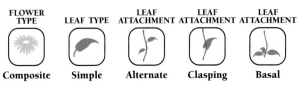

FLOWER TYPE	LEAF TYPE	LEAF ATTACHMENT	LEAF ATTACHMENT	LEAF ATTACHMENT
Composite	Simple	Alternate	Clasping	Basal

LITTLE SUNFLOWER
Helianthus pumilus

Family: Aster (Asteraceae)

Height: 12-32" (30-80 cm)

Flower: bright yellow, 2-3" (5-7.5 cm) wide, made up of tapered petals (ray flowers) surrounding a slightly raised center of deep yellow disk flowers

Leaf: lance-shaped, 2-4" (5-10 cm) long, covered with fine rough hairs, stalked, oppositely attached

Bloom: summer

Cycle/Origin: perennial, native

Zone/Habitat: foothills, montane; forest openings, fields, along roads, in meadows

Range: western half of Colorado

Notes: Little Sunflower, also known as Dwarf Sunflower, can grow somewhat tall. It may become rather bushy, thus it is sometimes referred to as Bush Sunflower. Although similar to other sunflower species in Colorado, this plant can be distinguished by its overall size and multi-stemmed branches. The tangled stems each give rise to one to three flowers. Genus name *Helianthus* comes from the Greek words for "sun" and "flower." The seed heads provide nutritional, late-season food for songbirds and small mammals.

FLOWER TYPE

Composite

LEAF TYPE

Simple

LEAF ATTACHMENT

Opposite

PRAIRIE SUNFLOWER
Helianthus petiolaris

Family: Aster (Asteraceae)

Height: 18-40" (45-102 cm)

Flower: bright yellow, 2-3" (5-7.5 cm) wide, made up of 10-24 petals (ray flowers) surrounding a raised, purplish-brown center of disk flowers

Leaf: narrowly lance-shaped, 3-6" (7.5-15 cm) long, covered with bristly hairs, on a stalk, alternately attached

Bloom: summer, early fall

Cycle/Origin: annual, native

Zone/Habitat: plains, foothills; fallow fields, along roads

Range: eastern half of Colorado

Notes: Alternately attached, long narrow leaves and purplish-brown disk flowers help to distinguish the Prairie Sunflower from many similar-looking wild sunflower plants. American Indians used this species extensively, and it may even have been cultivated. The seeds were eaten raw or cooked and were ground into a flour-like substance for cakes. Its large flower heads attract insect pollinators of all types, especially bees.

FLOWER TYPE	LEAF TYPE	LEAF ATTACHMENT
Composite	Simple	Alternate

BLACK-EYED SUSAN
Rudbeckia hirta

Family: Aster (Asteraceae)

Height: 1-3' (30-90 cm)

Flower: yellow, 2-3" (5-7.5 cm) wide, made up of 10-20 daisy-like petals (ray flowers) surrounding a button-like brown center (disk flowers); 1 to numerous large flower heads per plant

Leaf: slender, 2-7" (5-18 cm) long, very hairy, toothless, winged leafstalk clasps a hairy stem, alternately attached

Bloom: summer

Cycle/Origin: perennial or biennial, native

Zone/Habitat: plains, foothills, montane; dry soils, prairies, fields, open woods, along roads, in disturbed fields

Range: throughout

Notes: Also called Brown-eyed Susan, look for three prominent veins on each leaf and a characteristic winged leafstalk clasping each erect straight stem. Originally a native prairie plant in the plains, it is now also found in the foothills and montane life zones. The seeds are an abundant food source for small mammals and songbirds. Species name *hirta* is Latin for "hairy" or "rough," and refers to the plant's hairy nature. Just who Susan was remains unknown. American Indians sometimes used the young stems for food, but more often made tea from the roots to treat colds.

FLOWER TYPE	LEAF TYPE	LEAF ATTACHMENT	LEAF ATTACHMENT
Composite	Simple	Alternate	Clasping

HEARTLEAF ARNICA
Arnica cordifolia

Family: Aster (Asteraceae)

Height: 6-24" (15-60 cm)

Flower: bright yellow, 2-3" (5-7.5 cm) wide, composed of 8-10 petals (ray flowers) and many darker yellow disk flowers; 1-3 (usually 1) flowers found atop a single stem

Leaf: heart-shaped, up to 5" (13 cm) long, coarsely toothed, covered with velvety hairs

Bloom: summer

Cycle/Origin: perennial, native

Zone/Habitat: foothills, montane, subalpine; forests, shady slopes, moist areas

Range: western half of Colorado

Notes: Heartleaf Arnica is the only arnica in Colorado with heart-shaped leaves. Its flowers and leaves are much larger than those of Broadleaf Arnica (pg. 311). Spreads by horizontal underground stems (rhizomes), thus it is usually seen growing in patches. Genus name is from the Greek word *arnakis*, meaning "lambskin," and refers to the soft texture of the leaves. Because of the shape of the leaves, the Okanogan Indians considered the plant to be a love charm. They did not ingest the toxic leaves, but used them as a plaster to help heal cuts and bruises. Today, the leaves are used in some medicinal creams for sore muscles.

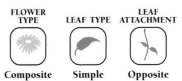

FLOWER TYPE	LEAF TYPE	LEAF ATTACHMENT
Composite	Simple	Opposite

BLANKETFLOWER
Gaillardia aristata

Family: Aster (Asteraceae)

Height: 1-2' (30-60 cm)

Flower: yellow, 2-3½" (5-9 cm) wide, made up of 10-20 petals (ray flowers) surrounding a dark red center (disk flowers); ray flowers have 3 notches at tips; sometimes petals have dark red bases that vary in size, making the flower appear red with yellow tips

Leaf: lobed, 3-6" (7.5-15 cm) long, basally attached, clasping the stem; fewer stem (cauline) leaves are smaller and alternately attached

Bloom: summer

Cycle/Origin: perennial, native

Zone/Habitat: plains, foothills, montane; in meadows and forest openings, hillsides

Range: throughout

Notes: This plant has flowers that look like red-eyed sunflowers. Blanketflower is easy to grow from seed and does well in gardens due to its tolerance to heat and drought. Numerous varieties are now cultivated throughout Colorado. Its flowers are popular for show, and its plant parts can be made into a tea to treat digestive problems or (supposedly) curb hair loss. Also an ingredient in a salve for saddle sores.

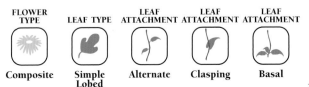

FLOWER TYPE	LEAF TYPE	LEAF ATTACHMENT	LEAF ATTACHMENT	LEAF ATTACHMENT
Composite	Simple Lobed	Alternate	Clasping	Basal

ORANGE SNEEZEWEED
Hymenoxys hoopesii

Family: Aster (Asteraceae)

Height: 2-4' (60-120 cm)

Flower: pale yellow to dull orange, 2-3½" (5-9 cm) wide, made up of drooping ray flowers with 3 lobes at tips surrounding a raised center of disk flowers

Leaf: lance-shaped, 4-12" (10-30 cm) long, alternately attached; stalked lower leaves are larger than the stalkless upper leaves

Bloom: summer

Cycle/Origin: perennial, native

Zone/Habitat: foothills, montane, subalpine; in moist mountain meadows, aspen groves

Range: western half of Colorado

Notes: "Sneezeweed" in the common name refers to sinus irritation the pollen can cause in some humans. Orange Sneezeweed grows in groups and produces many flowers, which attract butterflies, bees and moths. Its branched stems are stout and leafy. Although the roots have been used to treat some human ailments, it is not well liked by sheep ranchers. Sheep ingesting the plant can be affected with a type of poisoning called "spewing sickness." Also known as Owl's Claws.

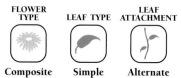

FLOWER TYPE	LEAF TYPE	LEAF ATTACHMENT
Composite	Simple	Alternate

ALPINE SUNFLOWER
Tetraneuris grandiflora

Family: Aster (Asteraceae)

Height: 2-12" (5-30 cm)

Flower: bright yellow, 2-4" (5-10 cm) wide, composed of 20-30 petals (ray flowers) surrounding a domed yellow center (disk flowers)

Leaf: lobed, 3-4" (7.5-10 cm) long, divided into numerous hairy lobes, basally attached

Bloom: summer

Cycle/Origin: perennial, native

Zone/Habitat: alpine; tundra meadows, among rocks, rocky slopes

Range: western half of Colorado

Notes: Alpine Sunflower is the largest and (some say) the most impressive of all the alpine wildflowers in Colorado. In fact, the species name *grandiflora* means "large flowered." In a year with favorable growing conditions, these sunflowers will delight tundra visitors with huge displays of color. Known by many common names such as Old-Man-of-the-Mountain, Sun God or Rydbergia. Also called Compass Flower because the flower heads face east all day; they do not follow the sun as commonly believed. The plant is covered with woolly hairs, which protect it from extreme alpine weather. Pollinated by insects, especially bees.

FLOWER TYPE

Composite

LEAF TYPE

Simple Lobed

LEAF ATTACHMENT

Basal

PLAINS PRICKLY PEAR
Opuntia polyacantha

Family: Cactus (Cactaceae)

Height: 8-48" (20-120 cm)

Flower: yellow (rarely red), 3" (7.5 cm) wide, made up of 5-12 overlapping petals surrounding a group of yellow flower parts (stamens); petals have a satiny sheen and texture

Leaf: fleshy oval green pad, up to 8" (20 cm) long, with clusters of spines

Fruit: flat-topped oval green fruit, turning purple to red, 2" (5 cm) long, fruit has numerous seeds

Bloom: spring, summer

Cycle/Origin: perennial, native

Zone/Habitat: plains, foothills; mesas, dry canyons, deserts, sunny slopes, shade intolerant

Range: western half of Colorado

Notes: A common cactus and one of the most cold tolerant known. Grown commercially in some parts of the world for its edible fruit and pads. Fruit can be eaten raw or dried; raw, it has a watermelon-like texture. Pads have minute barbed hairs that stick easily into the skin, causing considerable discomfort. As the grass is depleted on rangeland, these plants become more of a nuisance to cattle, whose faces and legs are irritated by cacti spines as they graze. However, pronghorn, deer, turtles and tortoises eat the fruit and pads.

FLOWER TYPE	LEAF TYPE	LEAF ATTACHMENT	FRUIT
Regular	Simple	Alternate	Berry

NODDING SUNFLOWER
Helianthella quinquenervis

Family: Aster (Asteraceae)

Height: 2-4' (60-120 cm)

Flower: bright yellow, 3-4" (7.5-10 cm) wide, composed of 12-20 petals (ray flowers) surrounding a raised, dark yellow-to-orangish center of disk flowers; nods on a single stalk

Leaf: lance-shaped, 10-16" (25-40 cm) long, leathery, 5 veins; leaves are mostly oppositely attached, a few basally attached; lower leaves are larger than upper

Bloom: summer

Cycle/Origin: perennial, native

Zone/Habitat: montane, subalpine; aspen forests, in meadows, on hillsides

Range: western half of Colorado

Notes: "Nodding" in the common name comes from the drooping flower, which appears as if it is bowing its head. Usually only one flower hangs from the stem, with the lower portion of the stem leafier than the upper. Species name *quinquenervis* refers to the five veins or "nerves" in the leaves, hence it is also known as Five-Nerved Sunflower. Look for the nodding flower head and the prominent veins in the leaves to distinguish this plant from other sunflower species. This plant grows in large clumps from spreading rootstock (rhizomes).

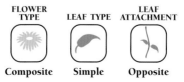

FLOWER TYPE	LEAF TYPE	LEAF ATTACHMENT
Composite	Simple	Opposite

ARROWLEAF BALSAMROOT
Balsamorhiza sagittata

Family: Aster (Asteraceae)

Height: 10-24" (25-60 cm)

Flower: bright yellow, 4" (10 cm) wide, composed of 12-25 petals (ray flowers) surrounding a darker yellow center, hairy green bracts in 2-4 rows around flower base; flower sits atop a leafless flower stem

Leaf: mostly arrowhead-shaped, up to 12" (30 cm) long and 6-8" (15-20 cm) wide, silver-gray, covered with felt-like hairs, basally attached

Bloom: spring, summer

Cycle/Origin: perennial, native

Zone/Habitat: plains, foothills, montane; fields, open hillsides, forests, mountain slopes

Range: throughout

Notes: The flowers of hundreds of these plants may color a field bright yellow during a growing season with favorable conditions. Species name is from the Latin *sagitta*, meaning "arrow," and refers to the shape of the leaves. The entire plant is edible and was once important to American Indians for food and medicine. The young leaves were eaten raw and tender shoots were used like celery–even the roots and seeds were consumed. Today, wildlife such as deer and elk feed on this plant.

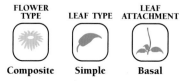

FLOWER TYPE — Composite

LEAF TYPE — Simple

LEAF ATTACHMENT — Basal

YELLOW POND-LILY
Nuphar lutea

Family: Water-lily (Nymphaeaceae)

Height: aquatic

Flower: bright yellow, cup-shaped, 3-5" (7.5-13 cm) wide, made up of 6-9 waxy petal-like sepals surrounding a yellow disk-shaped center (stigma); true petals are tiny, hidden below flower parts (stamens); flower is up to several inches above the water atop a stem

Leaf: round or heart-shaped, 4-14" (10-36 cm) wide, shiny green, deeply notched and anchored to long flexible stems; leaves float on the water

Fruit: green capsule, turning brown, 1-2" (2.5-5 cm) long; usually just above the surface of the water on a stem, occasionally floats; releases seeds into the water when mature

Bloom: summer

Cycle/Origin: perennial, native

Zone/Habitat: montane, subalpine; quiet shallow water, ponds

Range: western half of Colorado

Notes: Yellow Pond-lily is common in quiet or slow-moving water in high altitudes in Colorado. Roots produce large horizontal stems (rhizomes), which are buried in the mud at the bottom of a pond. Stout flexible vertical stems are attached to the stems. American Indians used the rhizomes for food. Also known as Spatterdock.

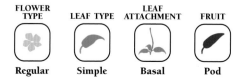

FLOWER TYPE	LEAF TYPE	LEAF ATTACHMENT	FRUIT
Regular	Simple	Basal	Pod

MULE'S EARS
Wyethia amplexicaulis

Family: Aster (Asteraceae)

Height: 12-30" (30-76 cm)

Flower: yellow, 4-5" (10-13 cm) wide, made up of 10-21 ray flowers surrounding a yellow center (disk flowers)

Leaf: elongated arrowhead-shaped, 10-20" (25-50 cm) long, glossy, hairless, alternately attached; lower leaves on short stalks, stalkless upper leaves

Bloom: spring, summer

Cycle/Origin: perennial, native

Zone/Habitat: montane, subalpine; in meadows, forest openings, on hillsides

Range: western half of Colorado

Notes: Named for the shape and size of the leaves, which resemble a mule's ears. This plant can be confused with Arrowleaf Balsamroot (pg. 353), which has hairy leaves. Look for the smooth glossy leaves of Mule's Ears to help identify. May grow profusely on hillsides in the Colorado mountains, usually west of the Continental Divide. Although ranchers do consider it a pest plant of grazing ground for livestock, domesticated animals generally avoid eating Mule's Ears. Wildlife such as deer and bear eat the early spring plants. American Indians once consumed the seeds, young shoots and cooked roots.

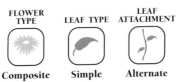

FLOWER TYPE — Composite   LEAF TYPE — Simple   LEAF ATTACHMENT — Alternate

COMMON SUNFLOWER
Helianthus annuus

Family: Aster (Asteraceae)

Height: 3-10' (90-300 cm)

Flower: sunny yellow, 3-6" (7.5-15 cm) wide, with 15-20 yellow petals (ray flowers) surrounding a large dark brown-to-purple center (disk flowers); each plant has 2-20 flowers

Leaf: triangular or heart-shaped, 3-7" (7.5-18 cm) long, stiff, coarsely toothed, alternately attached along a very coarse stem

Bloom: summer, fall

Cycle/Origin: annual, native

Zone/Habitat: plains, foothills, montane; dry soils, fields, along roads, open places, sun

Range: throughout

Notes: A smaller, wild version of Giant Sunflower, which is often cultivated in gardens and fields. Unlike the giant variety, the wild Common Sunflower usually branches several times, but still produces many nutritious seeds. Historically, used for food by many peoples. The seeds can be used to make flour, oil–even medicine. Often seen growing along highways, where the seeds of maturing plants are dispersed along the road by wind created from passing cars and trucks. Sunflowers do not follow the sun, as is widely believed. The flower heads face the morning sun once the plant matures and begins to bloom, thus most flowers face east.

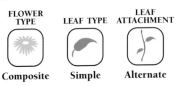

FLOWER TYPE	LEAF TYPE	LEAF ATTACHMENT
Composite	Simple	Alternate

ALPINE WALLFLOWER
Erysimum capitatum

Family: Mustard (Brassicaceae)

Height: 4-24" (10-60 cm)

Flower: round cluster, ½-1" (1-2.5 cm) wide, of deep yellow-to-orange flowers; individual flower, ½" (1 cm) wide, made up of 4 petals surrounding a group of flower parts (stamens)

Leaf: arrowhead-shaped or narrow, 1-3" (2.5-7.5 cm) long, slightly toothed, covered with fine hairs, basally and alternately attached

Fruit: long narrow green pod, turning brown, up to 3" (7.5 cm) long

Bloom: spring, summer

Cycle/Origin: perennial, native

Zone/Habitat: montane, subalpine, alpine; in forests, meadows, on rocky hillsides, mountain ridges

Range: western half of Colorado

Notes: A common plant growing in variety of habitats. Its height is determined by where it grows–plants in montane areas will be much taller than those found in the tundra. Seeds contain mustard oil, and American Indians used the oil to treat many ailments such as congestion, headache and intestinal worms. However, ingesting the oil in large amounts can be toxic. Species name *capitatum* means "head," and refers to the head-like shape of the flower clusters.

CLUSTER TYPE	FLOWER TYPE	LEAF TYPE	LEAF ATTACHMENT	LEAF ATTACHMENT	FRUIT
		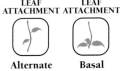			
Round	Regular	Simple	Alternate	Basal	Pod

CREEPING BARBERRY
Mahonia repens

Family: Barberry (Berberidaceae)

Height: 3-6" (7.5-15 cm); low shrub

Flower: tight round cluster, 1-2" (2.5-5 cm) wide, of many yellow flowers; individual flower, ¼" (.6 cm) wide, with 6 petal-like sepals and 6 petals, each in 2 whorls of 3

Leaf: compound, 8" (20 cm) long, alternately attached, composed of 5-7 leaflets; individual leaflet, 1-3" (2.5-7.5 cm) long, shiny, coarse-toothed edges, spiny tips, oppositely attached

Fruit: round green berry, turning purple, ¼" (.6 cm) wide; berries in grape-like clusters

Bloom: spring

Cycle/Origin: perennial, native

Zone/Habitat: foothills, montane; forests, fields, along fences

Range: western half of Colorado

Notes: A low shrub that produces yellow flowers as soon as the snow melts in early spring. Considered an evergreen since it retains its leaves all year, but the foliage commonly turns red in the fall. "Creeping" refers to the plant spreading by stems along and under the ground. Leaves and (sometimes red) stems look similar to those of the holly used in holiday decorating. The juicy berries are edible and can be used for jellies and wines. American Indians used its crushed roots for the antibacterial properties to help heal wounds.

CLUSTER TYPE	FLOWER TYPE	LEAF TYPE	LEAF ATTACHMENT	FRUIT
		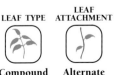		
Round	Regular	Compound	Alternate	Berry

AMERICAN YELLOWROCKET
Barbarea orthoceras

Family: Mustard (Brassicaceae)

Height: 1-2' (30-60 cm)

Flower: round cluster, 1-2" (2.5-5 cm) wide, of bright yellow flowers; each flower, up to ½" (1 cm) wide, has 4 petals

Leaf: lobed, 2-6" (5-15 cm) long, divided into 5-9 lobes; the end or terminal lobe is large and round; lower leaves are stalked, upper leaves clasp the stem

Fruit: cylindrical green pod, turning brown with age, 1-2" (2.5-5 cm) long

Bloom: spring, summer

Cycle/Origin: biennial, native

Zone/Habitat: plains, foothills, montane; moist sites, wet ditches and fields, irrigated pastures

Range: throughout

Notes: American Yellowrocket, also called Winter Cress, is one of three species of *Barbarea* found in the U.S. Some say it is toxic to animals if consumed in large quantities and advise humans to not eat the plant. Others say the leaves and stems can be eaten raw or cooked and add a radish-like flavor to foods. Enjoy this flower with your eyes and you will be sure to stay safe. Blooms early, providing color to spring fields. This is a host plant for the Green-veined White butterfly.

CLUSTER TYPE	FLOWER TYPE	LEAF TYPE	LEAF ATTACHMENT	LEAF ATTACHMENT	FRUIT
Round	Regular	Simple Lobed	Alternate	Clasping	Pod

365

ROUNDTIP TWINPOD
Physaria vitulifera

Family: Mustard (Brassicaceae)

Height: 4-10" (10-25 cm)

Flower: round cluster, 1-2" (2.5-5 cm) wide, of bright yellow flowers (usually some open, some closed); individual flower made up of 4 petals surrounding 6 flower parts (stamens)

Leaf: lobed and fiddle-shaped, 1-3" (2.5-7.5 cm) long, grayish green, hairy, basally attached; stem leaves are much smaller than basal leaves

Fruit: round-tipped green pod, turning light brown, up to ½" (1 cm) long; vertical groove on outside makes it seem like it is 2 "twin" pods joined together

Bloom: spring, summer

Cycle/Origin: perennial, native

Zone/Habitat: plains, foothills, montane; dry hillsides, along roads, canyons

Range: throughout

Notes: Blooms in early spring, producing many flowers even in a dry year. Prefers dry gravelly slopes. Flowers self-pollinate, but they also attract insects pollinators. Fourteen species of *Physaria* in the West, with Roundtip Twinpod the most common in Colorado. The shape and size of mature pod differentiates each species. "Roundtip" refers to the shape of the pod. Also called Fiddleleaf Twinpod.

CLUSTER TYPE	FLOWER TYPE	LEAF TYPE	LEAF ATTACHMENT	LEAF ATTACHMENT	FRUIT

Round	Regular	Simple Lobed	Alternate	Basal	Pod

MOUNTAIN PARSLEY
Pseudocymopterus montanus

Family: Carrot (Apiaceae)

Height: 10-24" (25-60 cm)

Flower: dense flat cluster, 1-2" (2.5-5 cm) wide, made up of tiny yellow flowers; cluster at the top of stem

Leaf: lobed, 2-6" (5-15 cm) long, deep lobes with pointed segments, on long stalk, basally attached

Bloom: summer

Cycle/Origin: perennial, native

Zone/Habitat: all life zones except plains; aspen groves, meadows, forest openings, hillsides

Range: western half of Colorado

Notes: Mountain Parsley is found in a variety of elevations–from the foothills all the way into the alpine life zone in Colorado. Its long taproot stores much energy for quick growth during the short growing season of higher elevations. Mountain Parsley has undergone several species name changes since botanist Asa Gray described this plant in the 1800s. The current species name *montanus* means "of the mountains." *Cymopterus* in the genus name comes from the Greek words for "winged" and "fruit." Also known as Alpine False Spring Parsley.

CLUSTER TYPE	FLOWER TYPE	LEAF TYPE	LEAF ATTACHMENT
Flat	Regular	Simple Lobed	Basal

ALPINE PAINTBRUSH
Castilleja puberula

Family: Snapdragon (Scrophulariaceae)

Height: 4-6" (10-15 cm)

Flower: spike cluster, 1-2½" (2.5-6 cm) long, of greenish yellow flowers hidden by woolly light yellow bracts

Leaf: narrowly lance-shaped, up to 3" (7.5 cm) long, alternately attached; upper leaves may be lobed

Fruit: pod-like green container, turning brown with age, ¾" (2 cm) long, contains many seeds

Bloom: summer

Cycle/Origin: perennial, native

Zone/Habitat: alpine; open slopes, ridges

Range: western half of Colorado

Notes: Alpine Paintbrush, also known as the Shortflower Indian Paintbrush, is the smallest species in the genus *Castilleja* found in Colorado. Only grows in high elevations, but the Alpine is not the only paintbrush species you will see at those altitudes. Frequently hybridizes with other paintbrush species, causing difficulty in distinguishing each. Look closely for the light yellow bracts to help identify the Alpine. Paintbrushes are semiparasitic, joining roots with those of neighboring plants to absorb nutrients. Thus, it is almost impossible to transplant paintbrushes to your garden and should not be attempted.

CLUSTER TYPE	FLOWER TYPE	LEAF TYPE	LEAF ATTACHMENT	FRUIT
Spike	**Tube**	**Simple**	**Alternate**	**Pod**

WESTERN INDIAN PAINTBRUSH
Castilleja occidentalis

Family: Snapdragon (Scrophulariaceae)

Height: 4-10" (10-25 cm)

Flower: spike cluster, 1-3" (2.5-7.5 cm) long, composed of inconspicuous green flowers hidden by showy greenish yellow bracts

Leaf: lance-shaped, 1-2" (2.5-5 cm) long, alternately attached

Fruit: pod-like green container, turning brown with age, ¾" (2 cm) long, contains seeds

Bloom: summer

Cycle/Origin: perennial, native

Zone/Habitat: montane, subalpine, alpine; meadows, hillsides, forest openings

Range: western half of Colorado

Notes: There are 150-200 species of paintbrushes throughout the West, with the Western Indian Paintbrush being one of the most common in the Colorado mountains. Those found growing in alpine elevations are much smaller than those growing in montane areas. Almost always found growing in clumps. Hybridization with other paintbrush species growing in the state makes positive identification difficult. Look for the unlobed simple leaves and greenish yellow bracts of Western Indian Paintbrush to help identify.

CLUSTER TYPE	FLOWER TYPE	LEAF TYPE	LEAF ATTACHMENT	FRUIT
Spike	Tube	Simple	Alternate	Pod

FENDLER GROUNDSEL
Packera fendleri

Family: Aster (Asteraceae)

Height: 10-18" (25-45 cm)

Flower: loose flat cluster, 1-3" (2.5-7.5 cm) wide, of yellow flowers; individual flower, ½-¾" (1-2 cm) wide, with drooping petals (ray flowers) surrounding a yellow button-like center (disk flowers)

Leaf: lobed, 2-4" (5-10 cm) long, narrow deeply cut lobes, pointed tips, mainly basally attached; smaller upper (cauline), alternately attached

Bloom: spring, summer

Cycle/Origin: perennial, native

Zone/Habitat: all life zones except plains; rocky slopes, on dry hillsides

Range: western half of Colorado

Notes: Fendler Groundsel (formerly Fendler Senecio) is in the genus *Senecio*, which contains over 2,000 species of groundsels and senecios worldwide. Many of these species have similar characteristics and are difficult to differentiate from each other. Look closely for the stalked, deeply lobed leaves to help identify. "Groundsel" is a derivative of the Anglo-Saxon word for "ground swallowing," referring to the ability of some groundsels to quickly spread and cover much ground. This species is named after the 1800s botanical collector Augustus Fendler.

CLUSTER TYPE	FLOWER TYPE	LEAF TYPE	LEAF ATTACHMENT	LEAF ATTACHMENT
Flat	Composite	Simple Lobed	Alternate	Basal

DWARF RABBITBRUSH
Chrysothamnus viscidiflorus

Family: Aster (Asteraceae)

Height: 12-18" (30-45 cm); shrub

Flower: flat cluster, 1-3" (2.5-7.5 cm) wide, of bright yellow flowers; each flower, ¼" (.6 cm) wide, consisting of disk flowers only

Leaf: thin and twisted, 1-2" (2.5-5 cm) long, grayish green, alternately attached

Bloom: summer

Cycle/Origin: perennial, native

Zone/Habitat: foothills, montane, subalpine; on dry hillsides, in open forests

Range: western half of Colorado

Notes: The most common of the Rabbitbrush species in western Colorado. Dwarf Rabbitbrush shrubs dot open western hillsides with bright yellow during the summer. Grows well in open deserts and among sagebrush flats. Rabbitbrush species vary considerably; Dwarf Rabbitbrush stems branch often and are hairless or only slightly hairy, not felt-like as in some species. The genus name *Chrysothamnus* comes from two Greek words, which when combined mean "gold bush." A host plant for Northern and Sagebrush Checkerspot butterflies. Also known as Yellow Rabbitbrush.

CLUSTER TYPE

Flat

FLOWER TYPE

Composite

LEAF TYPE

Simple

LEAF ATTACHMENT

Alternate

YELLOW STONECROP
Sedum lanceolatum

Family: Stonecrop (Crassulaceae)

Height: 4-8" (10-20 cm)

Flower: loose flat cluster, 1½-3" (4-7.5 cm) wide, of star-shaped yellow flowers; each flower, ½" (1 cm) wide, made up of 5 pointed petals, 5 pointed petal-like sepals and 10 flower parts (stamens)

Leaf: narrow, ½-1" (1-2.5 cm) long, light green, thick, fleshy, alternately attached

Bloom: summer

Cycle/Origin: perennial, native

Zone/Habitat: all life zones; dry open sites, among rocks

Range: throughout

Notes: Yellow Stonecrop occurs in all Colorado life zones–from the open plains of the prairies to the treeless tundra. Lower elevation plants will be larger than their alpine counterparts. It often grows in large groups, which form from horizontal rootstock (rhizomes). The stems and leaves are succulent, but should not be eaten since they can cause vomiting and diarrhea. Stonecrops are a favorite rock garden plant and are easily grown from cuttings. A host plant for Phoebus Parnassian and Moss Elfin butterflies.

CLUSTER TYPE	FLOWER TYPE	LEAF TYPE	LEAF ATTACHMENT
Flat	Composite	Simple	Alternate

RUBBER RABBITBRUSH
Ericameria nauseosa

Family: Aster (Asteraceae)

Height: 2-6' (60-180 cm); shrub

Flower: large round cluster, 1-4" (2.5-10 cm) wide, of bright yellow flowers; each flower, $\frac{1}{4}$-$\frac{1}{2}$" (.6-1 cm) wide, consisting of disk flowers only

Leaf: narrowly lance-shaped, 1-3" (2.5-7.5 cm) long, grayish green, alternately attached

Bloom: summer, fall

Cycle/Origin: perennial, native

Zone/Habitat: plains, foothills; dry slopes, along roads, in open forests and disturbed sites

Range: eastern half of Colorado

Notes: Most residents of Denver, the foothills and the plains know this colorful plant well. Rubber Rabbitbrush is very common and seems like it is growing in just about every flower garden or backyard. Individual shrubs sometimes get huge–up to 6 feet (1.8 m) tall and twice as big around. Aptly named, as many a rabbit will disappear under its branches. Large flower clusters attract all sorts of insect pollinators (especially beetles). American Indians made a dye from the flower heads for leather, baskets and dwellings. A host plant for Northern Checkerspot butterfly.

CLUSTER TYPE
Flat

FLOWER TYPE
Composite

LEAF TYPE
Simple

LEAF ATTACHMENT
Alternate

BLACKTIP RAGWORT
Senecio atratus

Family: Aster (Asteraceae)

Height: 12-32" (30-80 cm)

Flower: loose flat cluster, 1-4" (2.5-10 cm) wide, of yellow flowers; individual flower, ½" (1 cm) wide, made up of widely spaced 5-12 petals (ray flowers), raised dark yellow center (disk flowers) and green bracts with a conspicuous black tip

Leaf: lance-shaped, 4-10" (10-25 cm) long, basally attached and nearly vertical, upper (cauline), alternately attached; both leaf types covered with fine, woolly, grayish green hair

Bloom: summer

Cycle/Origin: perennial, native

Zone/Habitat: montane, subalpine; gravelly hills, along roads

Range: western half of Colorado

Notes: Blacktip Ragwort flowers add lots of yellow color to the montane and subalpine areas of Colorado. Even though it is a member of the extremely large *Senecio* genus (over 2,000 species worldwide), Blacktip Ragwort is fairly easy to identify. Often grows in large tall clumps containing perhaps hundreds of individual flowers. Look for the black-tipped green bracts just beneath the petals and for the woolly, almost vertical leaves. Attracts bees and butterflies, which pollinate the flowers in exchange for nectar.

CLUSTER TYPE	FLOWER TYPE	LEAF TYPE	LEAF ATTACHMENT	LEAF ATTACHMENT
Flat	Composite	Simple	Alternate	Basal

BROOM RAGWORT
Senecio spartioides

Family: Aster (Asteraceae)

Height: 1-2' (30-60 cm)

Flower: loose flat cluster, 2-3" (5-7.5 cm) wide, of yellow flowers; individual flower, 1" (2.5 cm) wide, made up of 6-12 widely spaced bright yellow petals (ray flowers) surrounding a yellow button-like center (disk flowers); clusters atop leafy stems

Leaf: thin and pointed, 2-4" (5-10 cm) long, alternately attached; when flowers are in bloom, leaves appear withered or dead on lower part of stems and thrive on upper portion

Bloom: summer

Cycle/Origin: perennial, native

Zone/Habitat: plains, foothills, montane; forest edges, along roads, open hillsides

Range: throughout

Notes: Broom Senecio is named for its numerous thin leaves on the upper portions of the stems–the plant looks similar to an inverted whiskbroom. Common along Colorado roadsides, especially along back roads where the soil has been disturbed. A member of the *Senecio* genus, one of the largest of the flowering plant genera. *Senecio* contains over 2,000 species, with about 50 in Colorado. Many people also know plants in this genus as "butterweeds," due to the color of the flowers and their abundance.

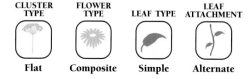

CLUSTER TYPE	FLOWER TYPE	LEAF TYPE	LEAF ATTACHMENT
Flat	Composite	Simple	Alternate

WESTERN GOLDEN RAGWORT
Senecio eremophilus

Family: Aster (Asteraceae)

Height: 1-2' (30-60 cm)

Flower: loose flat cluster, 2-4" (5-10 cm) wide, of yellow flowers; individual flower, ¾" (2 cm) wide, made up of 6-10 petals (ray flowers) widely spaced around a raised yellow center (disk flowers)

Leaf: deeply lobed, 2-4" (5-10 cm) long, pointed tips, alternately attached

Bloom: summer, fall

Cycle/Origin: perennial, native

Zone/Habitat: foothills, montane, subalpine; mountain slopes, along roads and trails

Range: western half of Colorado

Notes: Because there are so many similar-looking plants in the *Senecio* genus, it can be hard to identify your species. Look for wide spaces between the ray flowers and for deeply lobed leaves of Western Golden Ragwort. Species name *eremophilus* is from the Greek words *erem* and *philo*, which combine to mean "loving lonely places." This plant does well in disturbed areas such as along roads and newly constructed trails in the mountains. Western Golden Ragwort is chiefly pollinated by bees.

CLUSTER TYPE	FLOWER TYPE	LEAF TYPE	LEAF ATTACHMENT
Flat	Composite	Simple Lobed	Alternate

WHISKBROOM PARSLEY
Harbouria trachypleura

Family: Carrot (Apiaceae)

Height: 4-24" (10-60 cm)

Flower: flat cluster, 2-4" (5-10 cm) wide, made up of pale yellow flowers; each flower is tiny

Leaf: lobed, 4-10" (10-25 cm) long, divided into thin feather-like segments; leaves are mostly basally attached

Bloom: spring, summer

Cycle/Origin: perennial, native

Zone/Habitat: foothills, montane; in dry soils, openings in forests, canyon slopes, prairies

Range: western half of Colorado

Notes: "Whiskbroom" in the common name refers to the leaves, which are very thin and resemble the bristles of a whiskbroom. One of two common parsley species growing in Colorado. Can easily be distinguished from Mountain Parsley (pg. 369), which has wider leaves. Blooms early in spring and thrives in dry soil, sometimes with the flowers lasting for months. There are over 3,000 species in the Carrot family, which includes carrots, celery and other plants used for food. Several poisonous plants are also members of this family, including Poison Hemlock (pg. 269). Never consume any plant from the Carrot family unless you are positive you have identified it correctly.

CLUSTER TYPE	FLOWER TYPE	LEAF TYPE	LEAF ATTACHMENT
Flat	Regular	Simple Lobed	Basal

WESTERN WALLFLOWER
Erysimum asperum

Family: Mustard (Brassicaceae)

Height: 10-24" (25-60 cm)

Flower: loose round cluster, 2-4" (5-10 cm) wide, of yellow flowers; each flower, ¾-1" (2-2.5 cm) wide, with 4 round or oval petals; clusters at the end of stems

Leaf: very slender, 2-5" (5-13 cm) long, toothed, alternately attached; leaves are crowded on the stem

Fruit: slender green pod, turning brown, 3-5" (7.5-13 cm) long, 4-sided

Bloom: spring, summer

Cycle/Origin: biennial, native

Zone/Habitat: all life zones except alpine; in forest openings and meadows, prairies

Range: throughout

Notes: Western Wallflower is very common in Colorado and is the more eastern ranging of the wallflowers. Hybridizes with other wallflower species, resulting in plants with a range of colors and characteristics. This makes the Western Wallflower difficult to positively identify, but it usually has yellow (rarely orange) flowers. The plant has gone through numerous species name changes and is known by a host of common names. One such common name is Wormseed, from the American Indian practice of eating the bitter seeds to rid their stomachs of intestinal worms.

CLUSTER TYPE	FLOWER TYPE	LEAF TYPE	LEAF ATTACHMENT	LEAF ATTACHMENT	FRUIT

Round	Regular	Simple	Alternate	Basal	Pod

SULPHURFLOWER BUCKWHEAT
Eriogonum umbellatum

Family: Buckwheat (Polygonaceae)

Height: 4-12" (10-30 cm)

Flower: dense round cluster, 2-4" (5-10 cm) wide, of tiny bell-shaped yellow flowers; individual flower, ¼" (.6 cm) long

Leaf: spoon-shaped, 1-2" (2.5-5 cm) long, stalked, hairy underside, basally attached

Bloom: summer

Cycle/Origin: perennial, native

Zone/Habitat: foothills, montane, subalpine; forest openings, dry rocky slopes, along roads

Range: western half of Colorado

Notes: Sulphurflower Buckwheat plants can form clusters that, with sufficient moisture, can cover up to several square feet. The basal rosette of leaves gives rise to one woolly, usually leafless stem. Sometimes the stem has leaves just beneath the flower cluster. The characteristics of this species are highly variable due to the wide range of habitats and different life zones. A variety of wildlife such as chipmunks, birds and mice feed on the seeds.

CLUSTER TYPE	FLOWER TYPE	LEAF TYPE	LEAF ATTACHMENT
Round	Bell	Simple	Basal

YELLOW PEA
Thermopsis rhombifolia

Family: Pea or Bean (Fabaceae)

Height: 1-2' (30-60 cm)

Flower: loose spike cluster, 2-5" (5-13 cm) long, of bright yellow flowers; each flower, ½-1" (1-2.5 cm) long, pea-like, made of 5 petals (lips) fused together; clusters on upper portion of stems

Leaf: compound, divided into 3 oval leaflets and 2 leaflet-like stipules; each leaflet, ¾-1½" (2-4 cm) long; leaves are alternately attached

Fruit: green pod, turning brown, 1½-2¾" (4-7 cm) long, C-shaped and flattened

Bloom: spring, summer

Cycle/Origin: perennial, native

Zone/Habitat: all life zones except alpine; sandy soils, along roads, in meadows

Range: throughout

Notes: One of the earliest and brightest flowers to bloom at lower elevations in Colorado. Grows in large showy clumps that are hard to miss. Does well in rock gardens and can be easily grown from seed. The seeds should never be eaten, as they are poisonous. Range animals usually avoid this plant, thus it can sometimes overtake a grazing area. A host plant for Queen Alexandra's Sulphur and Persius Duskywing butterflies. Also called Prairie Thermopsis.

CLUSTER TYPE	FLOWER TYPE	LEAF TYPE	LEAF ATTACHMENT	FRUIT
Spike	**Irregular**	**Compound**	**Alternate**	**Pod**

PRAIRIE GROUNDSEL
Packera plattensis

Family: Aster (Asteraceae)

Height: 10-18" (25-45 cm)

Flower: loose flat cluster, 2-5" (5-13 cm) wide, of bright yellow flowers atop a woolly stem that branches near the top; each flower, ½-¾" (1-2 cm) wide, made up of 10-20 petals (ray flowers) surrounding a raised golden yellow disk

Leaf: lobed, oblong or oval, 4-8" (10-20 cm) long, woolly underside, basally attached; smaller upper (cauline), alternately attached

Bloom: spring, summer

Cycle/Origin: perennial or biennial, native

Zone/Habitat: plains, foothills; rocky soils, dry slopes, prairies

Range: eastern half of Colorado

Notes: Prairie Groundsel is a pretty, small plant with branching stems topped by loose flat clusters of bright yellow flowers. Spreads along horizontal underground stems (rhizomes) and, as a result, is usually found growing in clumps. Groundsels grow well in dry rocky soils and can be seen along eastern Colorado roads during the summer. The foliage is poisonous to livestock, but usually is not eaten frequently enough or in large enough quantities to cause problems. Sometimes called Prairie Ragwort. The genus *Packera* is named for John Packer, a modern-day Canadian botanist.

CLUSTER TYPE	FLOWER TYPE	LEAF TYPE	LEAF ATTACHMENT	LEAF ATTACHMENT
				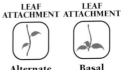
Flat	Composite	Simple Lobed	Alternate	Basal

ARROWLEAF RAGWORT
Senecio triangularis

Family: Aster (Asteraceae)

Height: 1-5' (30-150 cm)

Flower: loose open flat cluster, 2-6" (5-15 cm) wide, of bright yellow flowers; each flower, 1" (2.5 cm) wide, composed of 5-8 petals (ray flowers) and many yellow disk flowers

Leaf: elongated arrowhead-shaped or triangular, 3-8" (7.5-20 cm) long, coarse-toothed edges, alternately attached

Bloom: summer, fall

Cycle/Origin: perennial, native

Zone/Habitat: montane, subalpine; along streams, open areas near swamps, moist meadows

Range: western half of Colorado

Notes: Herbalists once believed smelling Arrowleaf Ragwort roots cured headaches; it is now known that this plant is toxic if eaten. Usually grows in clumps and is quite common in the wet areas of Colorado. "Arrowleaf" in the common name and the species name *triangularis* refer to the unmistakable shapes of the leaves. The fluffy seed heads resemble the white hair of an elderly gentleman, hence the genus name *Senecio,* which comes from the Latin word meaning "old man." In stories, fairies and witches used ragwort as their broomsticks.

CLUSTER TYPE	FLOWER TYPE	LEAF TYPE	LEAF ATTACHMENT
		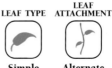	
Flat	Composite	Simple	Alternate

ROCKY MOUNTAIN GOLDENROD
Solidago multiradiata

Family: Aster (Asteraceae)

Height: 1-2' (30-60 cm)

Flower: spike cluster, 2-6" (5-15 cm) long, of yellow flowers; individual flower composed of 12-14 petals (ray flowers) surrounding as many as 30 yellow disk flowers

Leaf: elongated spoon-shaped, up to 4" (10 cm) long, smooth; mainly basally attached; fewer stem leaves are smaller and alternately attached

Bloom: summer, fall

Cycle/Origin: perennial, native

Zone/Habitat: montane, subalpine, alpine; open sites, sunny areas, slope, among rocks

Range: western half of Colorado

Notes: There is strong evidence to support claims by herbalists that Rocky Mountain Goldenrod has medicinal qualities. A tea made from goldenrods can be used to relieve stomach cramps and intestinal problems. Genus name *Solidago* is from the Latin word *solidus* and means "to make whole" or "to strengthen," referring to the healing powers of the plants. Pollinated by insects, not wind; thus this plant is not the cause of hay fever. A host plant for the Rockslide Checkerspot butterfly.

CLUSTER TYPE

Spike

FLOWER TYPE

Composite

LEAF TYPE

Simple

LEAF ATTACHMENT

Alternate

LEAF ATTACHMENT

Basal

BRACTED LOUSEWORT
Pedicularis bracteosa

Family: Snapdragon (Scrophulariaceae)

Height: 12-30" (30-76 cm)

Flower: spike cluster, 2-7" (5-18 cm) long, of pale yellow-to-light green flowers; each flower, 1" (2.5 cm) long, tubular, 2 petals (lips); lower lip is shorter than the upper lip

Leaf: compound, 3-12" (7.5-30 cm) long, divided into fern-like leaflets, alternately attached; each leaflet, 2-4" (5-10 cm) long, finely toothed

Bloom: summer

Cycle/Origin: perennial, native

Zone/Habitat: montane, subalpine; moist meadows, forest openings, rocky slopes

Range: western half of Colorado

Notes: Bracted Lousewort is a common plant most often spotted in moist areas in the Colorado mountains. Flower color is most often pale yellow, but it can be light green, green or maroon, depending upon growing conditions. Upper flower petal (lip) resembles the bow of an overturned canoe. Upper portions of the several unbranched stems have large flower clusters that attract bees and butterflies. Genus name *Pedicularis* is from a Latin word referring to lice, stemming from an ancient belief that animals would be infested with lice if they ate this plant.

CLUSTER TYPE	FLOWER TYPE	LEAF TYPE	LEAF ATTACHMENT
Spike	Irregular	Compound	Alternate

GIANT GOLDENROD
Solidago gigantea

Family: Aster (Asteraceae)

Height: 3-6' (90-180 cm)

Flower: spike cluster, 3-6" (7.5-15 cm) long, of small yellow flowers; each flower, ¼" (.6 cm) long, composed of 10-20 petals (ray flowers) surrounding a yellow center (disk flowers)

Leaf: lance-shaped, 2-6" (5-15 cm) long, toothed edges, pointed tip, alternately attached

Bloom: summer, early fall

Cycle/Origin: perennial, native

Zone/Habitat: plains, foothills; wet meadows, along streams

Range: eastern half of Colorado

Notes: There are several species of goldenrod in Colorado, and they can all look similar. Giant Goldenrod is one of the tallest, thus it is also known as Tall Goldenrod. It has smooth woody stems with many leaves. Can grow in tangled clumps, coloring the area yellow. Goldenrods are not the cause of hay fever (as many believe), since the pollen is not airborne. Flowers are pollinated by many types of insects. Also known as Late Goldenrod.

CLUSTER TYPE

Spike

FLOWER TYPE

Composite

LEAF TYPE

Simple

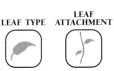

LEAF ATTACHMENT

Alternate

BUTTER-AND-EGGS
Linaria vulgaris

Family: Snapdragon (Scrophulariaceae)

Height: 1-2' (30-60 cm)

Flower: spike cluster, 3-6" (7.5-15 cm) long, of pea-like, yellow and orange irregular flowers; individual flower, 1" (2.5 cm) long, made up of 5 petals fused together like a snapdragon; a thin spur below each flower contains nectar

Leaf: thin, grass-like, 1-2" (2.5-5 cm) long, pale grayish green; upper leaves alternately attached, but leaves near base are sometimes oppositely attached

Bloom: spring, summer, fall

Cycle/Origin: perennial, non-native

Zone/Habitat: plains, foothills, montane; open fields, along roads

Range: throughout

Notes: Introduced from Europe, Butter-and-eggs escaped from gardens and now grows throughout Colorado, except in the sub-alpine and alpine life zones. Two-toned flower whose orange part, known as the "honey guide," acts like a target to guide insects into the long spur of the flower, ensuring the insect pollinates it before getting the nectar. A favorite of the hummingbird-like Sphinx Moth. Often grows in patches, reproducing along a horizontal underground stem (rhizome). Named after its yellow (butter) and orange (egg yolk) flowers. When flower is pinched, it opens wide like a frog's mouth, providing its other common name, Toadflax.

CLUSTER TYPE	FLOWER TYPE	LEAF TYPE	LEAF ATTACHMENT
	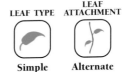		
Spike	Irregular	Simple	Alternate

TALL BUTTER-AND-EGGS
Linaria dalmatica

Family: Snapdragon (Scrophulariaceae)

Height: 2-4' (60-120 cm)

Flower: spike cluster, 3-6" (7.5-15 cm) long, of yellow and orange pea-like flowers near the top of a leafy stem; each flower, 1" (2.5 cm) long, made up of 5 petals fused together in snapdragon-like fashion; a long spur below each flower contains nectar

Leaf: broadly oval, 1-4" (2.5-10 cm) long, grayish green with pointed tips, alternate and clasping attachment

Fruit: cylindrical green capsule, ½" (1 cm) long; remains green well into fall

Bloom: early spring, summer

Cycle/Origin: perennial, non-native

Zone/Habitat: plains, foothills; open hillsides, along roads, disturbed soils

Range: eastern half of Colorado

Notes: Tall Butter-and-eggs can be differentiated from Butter-and-eggs (pg. 407) by its large, broadly oval leaves. This plant was introduced from Europe as an ornamental and now ranges throughout the West. Considered a noxious weed by Colorado state agricultural departments. Spreads by growing new shoots along a horizontal underground stem (rhizome) and producing many seeds. Also called Dalmation Toadflax.

CLUSTER TYPE	FLOWER TYPE	LEAF TYPE	LEAF ATTACHMENT	LEAF ATTACHMENT	FRUIT
Spike	Irregular	Simple	Alternate	Clasping	Pod

SMOOTH GOLDENROD
Solidago missouriensis

Family: Aster (Asteraceae)

Height: 12-16" (30-40 cm)

Flower: spike (sometimes flat) cluster, 3-8" (7.5-20 cm) long, of yellow flowers; individual flower, $\frac{1}{4}$-$\frac{1}{2}$" (.6-1 cm) wide, made up of 8-20 separated petals (ray flowers) that surround many yellow disk flowers

Leaf: thin, 3-6" (7.5-15 cm) long, smooth and leathery, alternately attached

Bloom: summer, early fall

Cycle/Origin: perennial, native

Zone/Habitat: plains, foothills, montane; along ditches and roads, rocky slopes

Range: throughout

Notes: A member of the genus *Solidago*, which contains numerous similar-looking species. Smooth Goldenrod is shorter than other goldenrods of the plains in Colorado. The smooth leathery leaves and the tight flower clusters, which can range in shape from spike to flat, also help distinguish this plant. Goldenrods typically grow in large clumps from spreading roots or runners. Contains a large amount of a latex-like substance, which someday could be an additional source for rubber. Some people eat the young leaves of goldenrod. Also called Missouri Goldenrod.

CLUSTER TYPE	FLOWER TYPE	LEAF TYPE	LEAF ATTACHMENT
Spike	Composite	Simple	Alternate

CANADA GOLDENROD
Solidago canadensis

Family: Aster (Asteraceae)

Height: 2-5' (60-150 cm)

Flower: mass of large arching spike clusters, 3-9" (7.5-22.5 cm) long; each spike made up of yellow flowers; each flower, ¼" (.6 cm) wide; tip of each spike usually nods to one side

Leaf: narrow, up to 6" (15 cm) long, rough to the touch, with sharp teeth; fewer leaves near base of stem

Bloom: summer, fall

Cycle/Origin: perennial, native

Zone/Habitat: plains, foothills, montane; dry soils, open fields

Range: throughout

Notes: This common plant, often seen in patches along roadsides, reproduces by sending up new plants from roots (clones). Creates patches 8-30 feet (2.4-9.1 m) wide, excluding other plants from the site. Over 100 types of goldenrod in North America, with over 10 in Colorado. All look similar and thus are hard to identify. While most yellow autumn flowers are a type of goldenrod and are often blamed for hay fever, most hay fever is actually caused by Ragweed (not shown). Only 1-2 percent of autumn airborne pollen is from goldenrod. Pollinated by insects such as flies, beetles, ambush bugs, midges and bees, which are attracted to the flower's abundant nectar. Stems are often invaded by insect larvae (usually a solitary wasp or fly larvae), causing large swellings (galls).

CLUSTER TYPE	FLOWER TYPE	LEAF TYPE	LEAF ATTACHMENT
Spike	Composite	Simple	Alternate

YELLOW SWEET CLOVER
Melilotus officinalis

Family: Pea or Bean (Fabaceae)

Height: 3-6' (90-180 cm)

Flower: spike cluster, 8" (20 cm) long, of yellow irregular flowers, ¼" (.6 cm) long

Leaf: compound, divided into 3 narrow, toothed, lance-shaped leaflets; each leaflet, ½-1" (1-2.5 cm) long

Fruit: ovate green pod, turning brown

Bloom: spring, summer, fall

Cycle/Origin: annual or biennial, non-native

Zone/Habitat: plains, foothills, montane; wet or dry soils, along roads, open fields, sun

Range: throughout

Notes: This non-native plant was introduced from Europe via Eurasia. Once grown as a hay crop, it has escaped cultivation and now grows throughout Colorado along roads and fields. The leaves and flowers when crushed smell like vanilla. Genus name *Melilotus* is Greek for "honey," referring to its use as a nectar source for bees. The rodenticide warfarin was developed from the chemical dicoumarin in sweet clover.

CLUSTER TYPE	FLOWER TYPE	LEAF TYPE	LEAF ATTACHMENT	LEAF ATTACHMENT	FRUIT

Spike	Irregular	Compound	Alternate	Basal	Pod

COMMON MULLEIN
Verbascum thapsus

Family: Snapdragon (Scrophulariaceae)

Height: 2-6' (60-180 cm)

Flower: club-like spike cluster, 1-2' (30-60 cm) long, of many small yellow flowers; each flower, ¾-1" (2-2.5 cm) wide, with 5 petals; flowers are packed along the stalk and open only a few at a time, from the top down

Leaf: large lower, 12-15" (30-38 cm) long, velvety with thick covering of stiff hairs; upper (cauline), stalkless, alternately attached, clasping the main stem; leaves progressively smaller toward top of stalk

Bloom: summer, fall

Cycle/Origin: biennial, non-native

Zone/Habitat: plains, foothills; dry soils, fields, along roads, sun

Range: eastern half of Colorado

Notes: A European import known for its very soft, flannel-like leaves, hence its other common name, Flannel Plant. This biennial takes two years to mature. The first year it grows as a low rosette of large soft leaves; in the second, a tall flower stalk sprouts. Its dried stems stand well into winter. It is said the Romans dipped its dried flower stalks in animal tallow to use as torches. Victorian women rubbed the leaves on their cheeks, slightly irritating their skin, to add a dash of blush. Early settlers and American Indians placed the soft woolly leaves in footwear for warmth and comfort.

CLUSTER TYPE	FLOWER TYPE	LEAF TYPE	LEAF ATTACHMENT	LEAF ATTACHMENT	LEAF ATTACHMENT
Spike	Regular	Simple	Alternate	Clasping	Basal

GLOSSARY

Alternate: A type of leaf attachment in which the leaves are singly and alternately attached along a stem, not paired or in whorls.

Annual: A plant that germinates, flowers and sets seed during a single growing season and returns the following year from seed only.

Anther: A part of the male flower that contains the pollen.

Basal: The leaves at the base of a plant near the ground, usually grouped in a round rosette.

Bell flower: A single, downward-hanging flower that has petals fused together, forming a bell-like shape. See *tube flower*.

Berry: A fleshy fruit that contains one or many seeds.

Biennial: A plant that lives for two years, blooming in the second year.

Bract: A leaf-like structure usually found at the base of a flower, often appearing as a petal.

Bulb: A short, round, underground shoot that is used as a food storage system, common in the Lily family.

Calyx: A collective group of all of the sepals of a flower.

Capsule: A pod-like fruiting structure that contains many seeds and has more than one chamber. See *pod*.

Cauline: The leaves that attach to the stem distinctly above the ground, as opposed to basal leaves, which attach near the ground.

Clasping: A type of leaf attachment in which the leaf base partly surrounds the main stem of the plant at the point of attachment; grasping the stem without a leafstalk.

Cluster: A group or collection of flowers or leaves.

Composite flower: A collection of tiny or small flowers that appears as one large flower, usually made up of ray and disk flowers, common in the Aster family.

Compound leaf: A single leaf composed of a central stalk and two or more leaflets.

Conifer: A type of plant that usually does not shed all of its leaves each autumn.

Corolla: All of the petals of a flower that fuse together to form a tube.

Deciduous: A type of plant that usually sheds its leaves each autumn.

Dioecious: Having male flowers on one plant and female flowers on another, never producing both sexes on the same plant.

Disk flower: One of many small, tubular flowers in the central part (disk) of a composite flower, common in the Aster family.

Ephemeral: Lasting for only a short time each spring.

Flat cluster: A group of flowers that forms a flat-topped structure, which allows flying insects to easily land and complete pollination.

Gland: A tiny structure that usually secretes oil or nectar, sometimes found on leaves, stems, stalks and flowers, as in Curlycup Gumweed.

Irregular flower: A flower that does not have the typical round shape, usually made up of five or more petals that are fused together in an irregular shape, common in the Pea or Bean family.

Leaflet: One of two or more leaf-like parts of a compound leaf.

Lip: The projection of a flower petal or the "odd" petal, such as the large inflated petal common in the Orchid family; sometimes, the lobes of a petal. See *lobe*.

Lobe: A large rounded projection of a petal or leaf, larger than the tooth of a leaf.

Lobed leaf: A simple leaf with at least one indentation (sinus) along an edge that does not reach the center or base of the leaf, as in Common Dandelion.

Margin: The edge of a leaf.

Monoecious: Having male and female flowers on the same plant.

Node: The place or point of origin on a stem where leaves attach or have been attached.

Nutlet: A small or diminutive nut or seed.

Opposite: A type of leaf attachment in which the leaves are situated directly across from each other on a stem.

Ovate: Shaped like an egg, with the larger end toward the stem.

Palmate leaf: A type of compound leaf in which three or more leaflets arise from a common central point at the end of a leafstalk, as in Silvery Lupine.

Parasitic: A plant or fungus that derives its food or water chiefly from another plant, to the detriment of the host plant.

Perennial: A plant that lives from several to many seasons, returning each year from its roots.

Perfoliate: A type of leaf attachment in which the bases of at least two leaves connect around the main stem so that the stem appears to pass through one stalkless leaf.

Petal: A basic flower part that is usually brightly colored, serving to attract pollinating insects.

Pistil: The female part of a flower made up of an ovary, style and stigma, often in the center of the flower.

Pod: A dry fruiting structure that contains many seeds, often with a single chamber. See *capsule*.

Pollination: The transfer of pollen from the male anther to the female stigma, usually resulting in the production of seeds.

Ray flower: One of many individual outer flowers of a composite flower, common in the Aster family.

Recurved: Curved backward or downward, as in bracts or sepals.

Regular flower: A flower with 3 to 20 typical petals that are arranged in a circle.

Rhizome: A creeping, (usually) horizontal, underground stem.

Rosette: A cluster of leaves arranged in a circle, often at the base of the plant, as in Common Mullein.

Round cluster: A group of many flowers that forms a round structure, giving the appearance of one large flower.

Saprophytic: A plant or fungus living on dead organic (plant) matter, neither parasitic nor making its own food, as in Pinedrops.

Seed head: A group or cluster of seeds.

Sepal: A member of the outermost set of petals of a flower, typically green or leafy, but often colored and resembling a petal.

Sheath: A tubular, leaf-like structure surrounding a stem, as in the American Bistort.

Simple leaf: A single leaf with an undivided or unlobed edge.

Spike cluster: A group of many flowers on a single, spike-like stem, giving the appearance of one large flower.

Spur: A hollow, tube-like appendage of a flower, usually where nectar is located, as in Colorado Blue Columbine.

Stamen: The male parts of a flower, consisting of a filament and an anther.

Stem leaf: Any leaf that grows along the stem of a plant, as opposed to a leaf at the base of a plant. See *cauline* and *basal*.

Stigma: The female part of the flower that receives the pollen.

Stipule: A basal appendage (usually in pairs) of a leaf that is not attached to the leaf blade, as in Yellow Pea.

Talus: The accumulation of many rocks at base of a cliff or mountain.

Taproot: The primary, vertically descending root of a plant.

Terminal: Growing at the end of a leaf, stem or stalk.

Throat: The opening or orifice of a tubular flower (corolla or calyx).

Toothed: Having a jagged or serrated edge of a leaf, resembling teeth of a saw.

Tube flower: A flower with fused petals forming a tube and usually turned upward, not hanging downward. See *bell flower*.

Umbel: A domed to relatively flat-topped flower cluster that resembles the overall shape of an open umbrella, common in the Carrot family.

Whorled: A type of attachment in which a circle or ring of three or more similar leaves, stems or flowers originate from a common point.

Woody: Having the appearance or texture resembling wood, as in stems, bark or taproots.

CHECK LIST/INDEX

Use the boxes to check wildflowers you've seen

DON MAMMOSER

Don Mammoser has been a full-time professional nature photographer and writer for ten years. He earned a Bachelor of Science degree in Zoology from the University of South Florida, which led to work for the U.S. Fish and Wildlife Service and as an endangered species researcher at the University of North Carolina. He teaches at photography schools and community colleges, and leads his own photography workshops. Don's publishing credits include *National Geographic Adventure*, *Popular Photography & Imaging*, *Outdoor Photographer*, *Nature's Best Photography*, *Audubon*, *Birder's World Magazine*, *Shutterbug*, *Ranger Rick* and many others. Don lives with wife Shelly and their children Sydney, Alex and Cassidy in Bailey, Colorado. He can be reached through his web site at www.donmammoserphoto.com.

STAN TEKIELA

Stan Tekiela is a naturalist, author and wildlife photographer with a Bachelor of Science degree in Natural History from the University of Minnesota. He has been a professional naturalist for more than 20 years and is a member of the Minnesota Naturalists' Association, Outdoor Writers Association of America and Canon Professional Services. He actively studies and photographs wildflowers and birds throughout the U.S. He received an Excellence in Interpretation award from the National Association for Interpretation and a regional award for Commitment to Outdoor Education. A columnist and radio personality, his syndicated column appears in over 20 cities, and he can be heard on a number of radio stations. He authors several field guides for other states including guides for birds, birds of prey, reptiles and amphibians, wildflowers and trees. Stan resides in Victoria, Minnesota, with wife Katherine and daughter Abigail. He can be contacted via his web page at www.naturesmart.com.

428